TRAINING AND SHOWING
THE VERSATILITY
RANCH HORSE

TRAINING AND SHOWING
THE
VERSATILITY
RANCH HORSE

by
LAREN SELLERS

THE LYONS PRESS
Guilford, Connecticut

The Lyons Press is an imprint of The Globe Pequot Press

The Lyons Press is an imprint of The Globe Pequot Press.

Material from the 53rd Edition of the AQHA Official Handbook of Rules and
Regulations and from www.aqha.com. Copyright © American Quarter Horse
Association. Reprinted with permission.

10 9 8 7 6 5 4 3 2 1

Printed in the United States of America

ISBN 1-59228-555-4

Library of Congress Cataloging-in-Publication Data
Sellers, Laren.
  Training and showing the versatility ranch horse / by Laren Sellers.
    p. cm.
  ISBN 1-59228-555-4 (trade cloth)
  1. Horses—Training. 2. Horses—Showing. 3. Versatility ranch
horse competitions. I. Title.
SF287.S43 2005
636.1'0835—dc22

                                         2005008553

DEDICATION

This book is dedicated to my daughter, Cydney.
May you learn to love unconditionally,
stay true to your word, and
know that no success can compensate for failure in the home.

CONTENTS

A Note from the Author

When I began working as a writer for the *American Quarter Horse Journal* in 2001, my horse experience was limited to working on my family's commercial cattle ranch in West Texas and perhaps showing one of our horses in a 4-H horse show in junior high. I was suddenly thrust into the horse show world, interviewing people who used terms I didn't recognize to discuss styles of competition that I didn't savvy.

Some of my first interviews for the *Journal* were with English riders who talked about finding someone to "band" their horses. Often, the person was a young girl who could earn extra money at the show. The only "banding" I knew concerned the castration of sheep and that was not often a money-making hobby for young girls. My learning curve was steep. That learning curve has been in place for a long time.

I remember roundup as an exciting time of year. Neighboring was the way ranchers were able to gather and brand their entire calf crop at once. One chilly morning after all the cowboys were mounted, Buster Cole was goaded into showing how his young horse could side pass. To the whistles of many appreciative cowboys, he tipped his hat. Without words they all knew that while side passing wouldn't be required of the horse much, the fact that he was supple-minded enough to perfect the skill was proof of a good horse. I was about eight years old or so, but it has always stuck in my mind that one of the positive components of a good ranch horse is its ability to be versatile.

It seems I took a good ranch horse for granted during my youth. This was made clear to me after returning from a weekend of shipping cattle. For years, I've taken photos of my family while on horseback when we gather and ship cattle. The days start early, usually in cold weather, with the crew sweeping pastures as the sun is coming up. Once at the pens with the cattle (usually around 10 a.m.) the sorting off of mother cows begins. My father is always in charge of that and his horses are quite skilled workers. Sorting is hard work. Afterward, I snapped a shot of my father letting his horse, Midnights Last (Dial At Midnight X Elliott Dutches), get a drink before the next stage of the day. It's one of my favorites, a sweaty ranch horse guzzling water from the concrete water tank. One of my colleagues at the *Journal* was amazed to see the horse drinking while still being bridled. I'd never thought about it as unusual and yet she had never seen it done before.

The saving grace in my writing career with the *Journal* came when the American Quarter Horse Association (AQHA) introduced the Versatility Ranch Horse (VRH) event in 2002. Finally, an event in which I felt more comfortable asking questions about the type horse I understood—a "usin' horse," and interacting with people I could relate to—cattle ranchers and their employees.

Please note that this book attempts to define some elements of the sport that can't be found in a *Webster's* dictionary. All definitions

My father's bay gelding, Midnights Last, gets a much needed drink after sorting the cows from the calves at our annual gathering in Andrews, Texas.

are accumulations of explanations I've heard through hours of interviews with horsemen and horsewomen who would rather work than be interviewed, rather show than tell. If a definition is slightly different from your understanding of the word, be lenient. Regional differences in handling horses can create individual interpretations.

Helping me create this book was my "in-house" editor and mother, Cindy Stroman, without whom I couldn't have attempted this book, and my favorite West Texas rancher, J. C. "Butch" Stroman, my father. Your assistance during this time in my life has been immeasurable. You are a perfect example of unconditional love and unending support. Thank you for raising me with a sense of humor and for reminding me that laughing at my own mistakes is often the only way to appreciate them. I appreciate you for putting up with me—the *&! #$%* Challenge.

I thank my sources, who all allowed me to interrupt their daily work in order to share with the public their love of the American Quarter Horse and their dedication to raising and training solid ranch horses. Thank you to the American Quarter Horse Association and, specifically, my coworkers from the *Journal*. My horse knowledge is greater, as is the list of my friends, because of each of you. I believe there is always room to increase both. I appreciate all of my friends outside the horse world who supported me and want a copy of this book even though they don't have any idea what I'm writing about. Thanks to my editor Steve Price for taking a chance on me as a first-time author. Thank you to my AQHA fact checker, Tawanna Walker, always gently correcting my errors. And to Jim Jennings, who recommended me to my editor as a writer for this book. Jim, I wanted to throw my hands up several times, but knowing that your name and your faith in me could be affected kept me on task. I hope you aren't disappointed with the outcome. You won't be surprised to hear I missed my first deadline.

Some things never change and some things never should.

TRAINING AND SHOWING
THE VERSATILITY
RANCH HORSE

CHAPTER 1
HISTORY OF THE SPORT

FOR CENTURIES, THE WORKING RANCH HORSE "COMPETITION" played out daily on ranches across America and Mexico, but it was simply thought of as putting in an honest day's work. Cowboys and breeders found pride in breeding and riding horses that could carry them through a tough day of ranch work. Industrialization and aggressive land development have all but done away with the cowboy way of life and use of the cow horse, but have not squelched the passion cowboys have for their useful horses. While many associations, including the American Quarter Horse Association and the American Paint Horse Association, have introduced events to showcase the talents of "using ranch horses," the skills displayed are not new. Cowboys have consistently relied on their mounts' versatility to help earn a living.

The new facet of this sport has moved the horse-and-rider team from the pasture to the show ring. AQHA's Versatility Ranch Horse event, which has seen exponential growth, was developed upon the requests of members who desired to demonstrate the talents of the working stock horse. Pulling from Foundation Quarter Horse events, the Ranch Horse Association of America (RHAA), which was organized to "promote the qualities and characteristics of the ultimate working ranch horse," and actual ranch work, AQHA developed five class distinctions to form the competition.

AQHA called on the top minds in the ranch horse world to put this event together. Bob Moorhouse, manager of the Pitchfork Land and Cattle Company in Guthrie, Texas; Jim Heird, associate dean of the College of Agricultural Sciences at Colorado State University; Joe Wolter, horse trainer and cattle rancher, Aspermont, Texas; B. F. Yeates, Stock Horse of Texas executive secretary; and Alex Ross, chairman of AQHA's Judges Committee, met October 24, 2000, to brainstorm the idea of a ranch horse contest. During the next seven months, the original task force members mulled over ways to implement a successful ranch horse class. Then in June 2001, the group met again along with Gary Fields of the Texas Foundation Quarter Horse Association and in-house AQHA staff executive vice president Bill Brewer, executive director of shows and regional services Cam Foreman, senior director of shows Charlie Hemphill, senior director of marketing Tom Persechino, director of information technology Jim Savage, director of judges Billy Steele, and executive director of marketing and membership services Don Treadway to develop the American Quarter Horse Association's Versatility Ranch Horse Competition.

Implemented in January 2002, the inaugural Versatility Ranch Horse contest took place at the Southwestern Exposition and Livestock Show in Fort Worth, Texas, on January 12, 2002. The contest featured fifteen entries including those owned by four AQHA/Bayer Best Remuda Award winners. The Four Sixes Ranch of Guthrie, Texas, took top honors with Little Playgun. The four-year-old gray mare (Playgun X Little Brim by Peppy San Badger) was ridden by Joe Wolter. The pair won the competition with a total of thirty-five points, placing first in the working ranch horse and mare conformation events, second in ranch riding and ranch cutting, and third in ranch trail.

The W. T. Waggoner Estate of Vernon, Texas, placed second with Borregos Double (Docs Borrego X Miss Double 127 by Double Bid Man) with twenty-nine points. Wes O'Neal rode the seventeen-year-old bay gelding to three third-place finishes in ranch cutting, ranch riding, and gelding conformation, and second place in ranch trail.

Joe Wolter piloted four-year-old mare Little Playgun (Playgun X Little Brim) for the Four Sixes Ranch to win the inaugural AQHA Versatility Ranch Horse competition January 2002, in Fort Worth, Texas. Wolter accepts the Lisa Perry bronze trophy from AQHA President J. D. Blondin.
(Photo courtesy of the *American Quarter Horse Journal*.)

Third place went to the Pitchfork Land and Cattle Company with Sir Seventy Four. Sir Seventy Four was sired by Sirs Sir and out of Miss FF Fork. Mark Voss rode the four-year-old dun gelding to earn twenty-five points. Sir Seventy Four was named overall conformation champion. Ima Eddie Hancock, owned by the R. A. Brown Ranch of Throckmorton, Texas, placed fourth under the hand of George Self. The gray gelding, who is by Hesa Eddie Hancock and out of Ima Gold Rock, won the ranch riding class to earn twenty-one points. Kevin Gursky of Jacksboro, Texas, showed his three-year-old bay stallion, Joe Don Hancock, to win the ranch trail competition and fifth place overall with twenty points. Joe Don Hancock is by Red Rooster Hancock and out of Hot Fudge Hancock.

An eager audience packed the stands of the expo center in Fort Worth for the debut. The event's instantaneous popularity revealed that the Versatility Ranch Horse competition filled a niche that had not been addressed by the association's other classes.

"For many horse enthusiasts, the Quarter Horse's ability to do many things well is the most logical reason to own one," Charlie Hemphill, AQHA senior director of shows, says. "Our aim was to keep that in mind as we outlined what would be included in the Versatility Ranch Horse competition. It has brought back a group of people that had quit showing in AQHA. These were the exhibitors who once showed a single horse in cutting, Western pleasure, and conformation. When people started specializing horses to specific events, a select type of exhibitor drifted out of the arena. They were still riding good horses, but didn't have a place where they fit. Versatility Ranch Horse competition gave them a place to show their horses in many events that showcased the versatility of their horses. On another level, it has provided an opportunity for people to take part in the Western lifestyle. Not all of the competitors are ranch cowboys, but they respect the Western way of life and can participate in it.

"People expect this type horse to be from one of the many legendary ranches in Texas, Oklahoma, Nebraska, Wyoming, or Nevada," Hemphill says. "But our year-end high-point horse in 2004 was from Pennsylvania. Versatility Ranch events cross all stereotypical boundaries and open the door to horse enthusiasts from every walk of life."

Year-End High-Point Horse
An award given to any horse in the Open division or any single horse/exhibitor combination in the Amateur or Youth divisions based on the total number of points earned during a calendar year in each AQHA-approved event in which points are awarded.
—*www.aqha.com*

The Versatility Ranch Horse competition demonstrates the versatility of the working ranch horse in five categories: ranch riding, ranch trail, ranch cutting, working ranch horse, and ranch conformation. To be eligible for points in the Versatility Ranch Horse competition, a single horse and rider duo must enter all five classes. Credits are applied per class according to the placing received based on the number of horses competing in that particular class. Horses competing and placing in the top nine are awarded one credit for each horse or contestant placing below them, plus one credit. Total credits will not exceed nine credits for first place. Credits received in each class will be totaled. After totaling, the horse receiving the highest number of credits will be placed first in the Versatility Ranch Horse competition. The horse receiving the second highest credits will be placed second in the Versatility Ranch Horse competition and so on. AQHA points are awarded in the versatility ranch class according to the existing point schedule (Chart 415A of the AQHA Official Handbook of Rules and Regulations). Ties in the final placing for the Versatility Ranch Horse competition are broken by the highest-placing horse in the working ranch class. All exhibitors in the working ranch class should be placed to break ties.

This example, provided by AQHA, represents a class with six contestants. Refer to the AQHA Official Handbook of Rules and Regulations for more information on the credit distribution for classes.

EXAMPLE OF CREDIT DISTRIBUTION
(Courtesy of the American Quarter Horse Association)

Contestant Versatility Number	Ranch Riding	Ranch Cutting	Ranch Trail	Working Ranch	Conformation	Total Credits	Placing	Points
#233	6	4	5	6	5	26	1	1
#285	3	3	6	5	4	21	2	½
#289	5	5	2	2	6	20	3	0
#186	2	6	1	4	2	15	4	0
#222	4	1	4	3	1	13	5	0
#193	1	2	3	1	3	10	6	0

DIVISIONS—OPEN AND YOUTH

The open division is for horses shown by the recorded owner, by immediate family members, or by a full-time employee of the owner, provided the employment has covered at least six months.

The youth division covers exhibitors eighteen years of age or younger as of January 1, given that they are the recorded owner or exhibit a horse owned by an immediate family member. Youth exhibitors are allowed to show horses owned by a ranch that employs the exhibitor's family full-time. The full-time employment must have been for six or more months prior to the show.

For a person to show a horse in Versatility Ranch Horse competition in which the exhibitor is not the current listed owner, the exhibitor must contact AQHA for preapproval procedures. The exhibitor will need to complete an application to verify that he or she derives at least 70 percent of total income from employment with the recorded owner of the horse. The exhibitor must receive approval to show the employer's horse before the date of the show.

An AQHA Year-End High-Point award is presented in both the ranch and youth divisions based on the number of points earned from January 1 to December 31 of each year.

- All achievements are included on horses' show records and exhibitor/owner award records.
- Awards at individual shows may vary.
- Owners of horses enrolled in the Incentive Fund are eligible to receive money earned based on total versatility ranch points earned during the year. Sires of horses competing in the Versatility Ranch Horse competition that are Incentive Fund-nominated also can earn yearly dividends for their owners.

For a more detailed explanation, refer to the AQHA Official Handbook of Rules and Regulations pertaining to the year you will show, or contact AQHA's customer service department at 806-376-4811.

CLASSES

Ranch riding displays the horse's ability to move at a working speed under the rider's hand by showing at three gaits: walk, trot, and lope. Exhibitors are asked to use all gaits in both directions, change directions on the rail, stop, and back. According to AQHA.com,

> *A horse will be given credit for traveling with his head held in a normal position, ears alert and moving at a natural speed for the gait requested. Horses will be asked to extend the lope and the trot in at least one direction. Credit also will be given for making a smooth transition between the gaits, for keeping the correct lead and for maintaining the gait until the judge asks for a change. A rider must show his horse with only one hand on the reins, unless the horse is 5 years old or younger and is being shown in a snaffle bit, hackamore or bosal.*

Ranch trail contains a course with a minimum of six obstacles and is designed to show a horse's ability and willingness to perform several tasks that might be asked of it during the course of a normal day's ranch work. Some shows incorporate the landscape into the trail course, abiding by AQHA's request that natural obstacles be used whenever possible.

The horse is judged at the walk, trot, and lope performed between the six obstacles as determined by the judge when the pattern is selected. A horse will be rewarded with higher credit for performing these gaits on the correct lead and with an alert attitude. Mandatory obstacles include opening, passing through and closing a gate, and dragging a log either in a straight line or around a set pattern. The third mandatory obstacle requires the

Using only one hand to rein and minimal visual cues to transition from one gait to the next will result in your best possible score during the ranch riding class.

During the 2002 Best of the Remudas Versatility Ranch Horse Competition Circuit, the Four Sixes Ranch constructed an unusual ranch trail class that began with exhibitors crossing a bridge and then walking down a steep slope before completing the other aspects of the course. This provided realistic terrain for the competitors and an inviting visual change for spectators.

Trotting across logs is a common ranch trail obstacle, here negotiated by Vince Neal and his 1997 gray stallion MC Starbert Hancock (Starbert Star Leo X Sweet Sue 1990) during an Oklahoma competition.

Practicing this mandatory ranch trail class obstacle helped Janiejill Tointon, of Longmont, Colorado, judge how much length of rope to allow as slack before approaching and circling a cone on palomino mare Shiners Spumanti (Shining Spark X Taris Vintage).

horse to remain quiet while the rider dismounts, removes the bit completely from the horse's mouth, rebridles, and then picks up all four of the horse's feet. Some optional obstacles include crossing a water hazard, being hobbled or ground tied, and crossing a bridge.

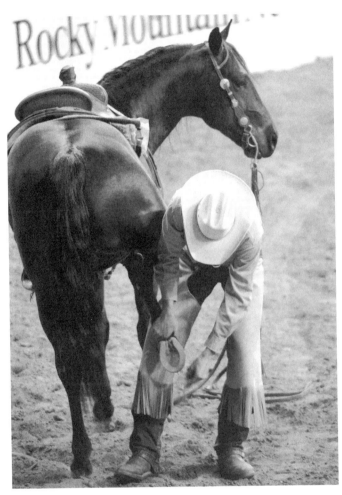

A gentle horse allows all feet to be picked up and examined. This is helpful for trimming, shoeing, and cleaning the foot, as demonstrated by Cody Crow with bay stallion Amigos Medicine (Chics Medicine Man X Amigos Cutter) in Denver.

In **ranch cutting** a single, numbered cow is cut from the herd and the horse must demonstrate its ability to work the cow. Contestants will have two and one-half minutes to cut and pen a designated cow from a herd of at least ten head. The exhibitor will have two turn-back riders helping to keep the cow at the set end of the arena. When satisfied that the horse has proven its cutting ability, the horse and rider must then pen the cow at the far end of the arena. Horses will not be penalized for reining during the cutting portion but should display the horse's natural cow ability.

Natural Cow Ability

A horse with natural cow ability responds to the movement of a cow with a balanced, smooth reaction. When a horse can outthink the cow, it is displayed through short bursts of speed, midair pivots, and fabulous footwork. Ears will be alert and the horse will watch the cow separated from the herd, often lowering its nose to get eye level with the cow.

Katherine Lyons and bay mare Sliks Sweet Tart (Playboys Slik Lena X Miss Peppy Tart) successfully separate a cow from the herd during the ranch cutting class of a VRH competition in Woodward, Oklahoma.

Mike Major, of Fowler, Colorado, turns a cow on the fence with 1999 sorrel stallion Dynamite Bravo Doc (Doc O Dynamite X Starlite Missy Bravo). Dynamite Bravo Doc placed in the top ten high-point standings in VRH in 2003 and 2004.

The **working ranch horse** class combines the ability of the working ranch horse to rein, handle cattle, and put its rider in the position to rope and stop a cow. Each contestant performs individually. The class is judged in three sections—reining, cow work, and roping—with scores from each section added together for the final score of the class. An average score for the entire class would be 210 points with each section—reining, cow work, and roping—counting for 70 points. If a contestant fails to attempt any required portion of the class, the result will be a zero score for the entire class. A maximum of six minutes is allowed to complete the class. When the six-minute time limit has expired, the exhibitor is required to exit the arena.

Reining pattern: one of two approved patterns will be used for this class. Maneuvers include at least one circle in both directions, a change of leads in each direction, at least one 360-degree turn in each direction, a rollback in each direction, stop, and back. Refer to the most recent copy of the AQHA Official Handbook of Rules and Regulations for any pattern alterations.

During the cattle classes, a judge may award an exhibitor new cattle to exhibit the horse's ability based on the following criteria:
1. The cow won't or can't run.
2. The cow won't leave the end of the arena.
3. The cow is blind or won't yield to the horse.
4. The cow leaves the arena.
—*2005 AQHA Official Handbook of Rules and Regulations*

The cow shown here would represent one that an AQHA Versatility Ranch Horse competition judge could excuse and replace with new stock under the four criteria AQHA has in place.

Working the cow: after the exhibitor has completed his reining pattern, he will call for the cow to be turned into the arena. Upon receiving the cow, the contestant shall hold the cow on the prescribed end of the arena for a sufficient amount of time to demonstrate the ability of the horse to contain the cow. After a reasonable amount of time, the contestant shall take the cow down the fence, making at least one turn each way on the fence.

Roping: the exhibitor must then rope the cow and bring it to a stop. The horse is judged on its ability to trail, rate, and stop the cow. There is to be no dragging and the exhibitor is allowed only two throws. Any catch that holds the animal is considered legal. Ropes cannot be tied to the saddle horn. It's not necessary for the exhibitor to catch in order to receive a score. However, if there is no catch, a five-point penalty is subtracted from the roping score.

Ranch conformation is based on balance, structural correctness, breed and sex characteristics, and degree of muscling; however, balance carries most weight in the judging process. Horses are to be shown in a good working halter (rope, braided nylon, or plain leather). Horses will walk to the judge one at a time. As the horse approaches, the judge will step aside to allow the horse to trot straight to a cone placed fifty feet away. At the cone, the horse will continue trotting, turn to the left, and trot toward the left wall or fence of the arena. After trotting, horses will be lined up head to tail for the judge to complete an individual inspection. The judge shall inspect each horse from both sides, front and rear, and place the horses according to preference. The ranch conformation class will be held after the conclusion of the other four events. All sexes will be shown together as one class.
Ranch division: stallions, mares, and geldings
Youth division: mares and geldings

Carries Dreamer (Skip A Dreamer X Carrie Michelle 84 [TB]) and Michael Alumbaugh, of Los Lumas, New Mexico, exhibit a nice example of the good working halter encouraged by AQHA for the ranch conformation class.

TACK

Saddles

It is unusual to glimpse many exhibitors riding silver-free saddles at Western horse shows these days. However, AQHA encourages exhibitors in VRH to use a working outfit for showing purposes. "Many of these competitors don't show their horses for a living," Charlie Hemphill says. "We want them to feel comfortable saddling their horses like they would as they head out to gather cattle or ride fences. This event is to show off what the horse and rider can do as close to their natural environment as we can get."

If you are purchasing a new saddle, look for one built for hard use and one that is comfortable for you and for your horse. Saddles can be basic or customized, depending on your budget. You'll be pulling a log and roping a calf. Consider the pressure that will be put on your saddle. Many saddles currently used in VRH are a combination of saddles created for roping, cutting, and reining. This type saddle has a narrow, semiflat seat, and a reinforced saddle horn. Both rough-out and smooth-seated saddles are used in VRH, based on personal preference. Ask an experienced trainer or saddle maker to help determine your horse's needs before purchasing a saddle. A proper-fitting saddle will extend the health of your horse and make competition more enjoyable for you both.

Saddle Pads and Cinches

Most exhibitors choose saddle pads and cinches with natural fibers. Wool and mohair are two such fibers that will absorb sweat, wicking it away from your horse. During a long day of showing, this helps keep your horse comfortable. Also, wool is one of several natural fibers that has the ability to last through years of use with proper care. Be aware that some neoprene-type saddle pads and cinches can keep heat from escaping the saddled horse and thus cause soreness.

In the top photo, this saddle used by Kim Lindsey on Double Plus Freckles (Dont Boss Me Around X Bellamac) represents a typical tooled-leather saddle seen in VRH competitions in many western states, although variations occur throughout different regions. Below, Tim Ettleman, of Longmont, Colorado, chooses to show his sorrel mare Ima Peppy Poco Candy (Pine Oh Mite X Silky Baby San) in a rugged working saddle in a Denver event.

Some VRH shows extend beyond one day and any soreness or stiffness could prevent your horse from showing to its full potential.

Inexpensive nylon off-billets and tie straps might be tempting because of the reasonable price, but our sources say leather is still the way to go. Leather provides necessary stretch to maintain your horse's comfort.

Before each ride, double-check your cinches for any weaknesses and replace what needs replacing.

Headstalls and Halters

Kim Lindsey, a trainer and competitor with the Box P Ranch in Jayton, Texas, agrees that most working outfits are a natural fit for the VRH competitor. "When it comes to the saddle and bridles, the rule book discourages a lot of silver," she says. "Most of the competitors you see ride something that they would ride working on the ranch. It's not logical to ride a saddle with silver in the brush we have and to me, it's not logical to ride a saddle loaded with silver in a ranch horse contest. I think the whole idea is to keep the attention on the horse. The goal is to see how the horse and rider perform in the tack and situations that are as close to the ranch as possible."

During the conformation class, a plain leather, nylon, or rope halter is acceptable. Simplicity is key when choosing a headstall. Lindsey recommends a traditional headstall with a brow band and throatlatch. Selecting a bit will depend on your horse. She says a snaffle bit is common, but it is important to practice in a bit you can show in. Double-check the AQHA rules concerning VRH if you have concerns. Practicing with a bit that is illegal and then changing bits the day of the show is likely to make your day at the show less than enjoyable.

Leg Protection

Fast-moving classes, like working ranch horse and cutting, mean that you need to protect your horse's legs. Bell boots and splint boots are a convenient way to avoid injuries.

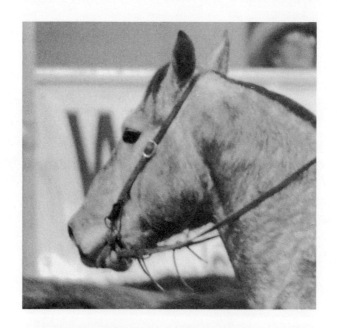

Headstalls can range from the ultra simple (top) as seen on gray stallion Hancock Star Beam (Star Beam Snip X Hancock Bar 022) to the more decorative. The bottom headstall was worn by sorrel gelding Colonels Lemac (Colonel Wisp X Ladybars Lemac).

"The only thing that might be different going to a show is that I will put boots on one at the show for preventative measures," says Stuart Ranch horse division manager and trainer Chris Littlefield of Waurika, Oklahoma, who was the 2002 Best of the Remudas Versatility Ranch Horse Circuit Champion. "That's not a feasible piece of equipment when riding here at home because of all the stickers we'd be picking out of them after ten minutes in the pasture. Make sure that everything you expect to show in is AQHA-legal."

ATTIRE

Most exhibitors ride wearing plain leather chaps over dark blue denim jeans with the boots and spurs customary to their region. A hat and long-sleeved shirt are always worn, with jackets or vests determined by weather conditions. In keeping with the feel of the event, clothing should be suitable for ranch work and steer clear of anything that looks like a costume. Again, the goal is to show off the horse's ability to work as a natural partner, not to display your appreciation for sequins and rhinestones.

General Rules

- All horses must be registered with the American Quarter Horse Association.
- Each exhibitor must have current individual membership in the American Quarter Horse Association or American Quarter Horse Youth Association (AQHYA).
- No horses less than three years of age may be exhibited.
- No hoof polish.
- No braided or banded manes.
- No tail extensions.

- Trimming the inside of ears is discouraged.
- Trimming the bridle path is allowed, as well as the fetlocks or any excessive (long) facial hair.

The Grassroots Creation of RHAA

As told in the November 2001 Lone Star Horse Report:

One day in March, 1995, Bill Smith and his neighbor Phil Guitar were branding calves when they began to discuss the idea of a West Texas ranch horse contest. In just two months, assisted by Mike Seago (then of The Four Sixes), Bob Moorhouse of the Pitchfork Land and Cattle Company, and Tom Moorhouse of Moorhouse Ranch, they put together their first competition of reining, roping and cow work at the Western Heritage Classic Ranch Rodeo in Abilene.

In 1998, with the help of attorney Kelly Gill, they organized the Ranch Horse Association of America "to promote the qualities and characteristics of the ultimate working ranch horse."

At the end of last year (2000), the RHAA had approximately 250 members and continues to add new ones at every show. This year, the group has sanctioned 18 working ranch horse competitions in Texas, Oklahoma, Kansas, Wyoming and Arizona. Next year's schedule includes shows in New Mexico and Nebraska. The National Finals, now limited to the top 50 qualifiers, are held during the Western Heritage Classic in May.

CHAPTER 2

SELECTING THE COMPETITIVE HORSE

THE KEY TO SUCCESS IN THE VERSATILITY RANCH HORSE competition is finding a horse that can display quality characteristics in each of the diverse array of classes. Therefore, the selection of such an animal deserves important consideration. You will desire a horse that has talent and has the heart to compete. You will desire a horse that has eye appeal. You might desire a horse that you have bred and raised to show off your broodmare's quality traits. In a perfect world, you will already own this phenomenon all wrapped up in one horse. If not, you will need to search for one to purchase.

In either case, one of the attractions of VRH is that one only needs a single horse to compete in multiple events. "It has a draw for people that might not own a ranch or work on a ranch because they can compete on one horse in several events," Stuart Ranch manager Chris Littlefield says. "Versatility Ranch Horse shows are a day filled with events that are fun to watch. It naturally becomes a family day.

"The ideology takes us back to what AQHA was founded on—a horse you could do anything on," he continues. "You could do the trail; they were a pleasure to ride as far as being smooth travelers and yet, they could work a cow, go down a fence, set you up to rope, or pull a log. That's the whole idea. I think it is a great way to revert to the original. Horses are bred to be so specialized now. I think many people have lost sight of the value of having a horse that is conformationally correct,

because a horse with correct conformation should naturally be an out-standing performer."

The VRH competition was designed for the American Quarter Horse breed, which won the hearts of horse people because of its natural versatility. A well-bred Quarter Horse has speed, agility, stamina, and cow sense. While many events now focus on training specialization, this event lends itself to displaying the gamut of the breed's talent.

"The thing about the Versatility Ranch Horse is that you can take a ranch horse and show it and you are doing the same thing that you would on the ranch," says Littlefield. "You don't have to have a lot of special tack. You don't have to have the most special horse, but if it is a good all-around horse and can earn points in several events, by the end of the day, you can still place in the competition. That's exactly why Terry Stuart Forst and I decided to show 'Miss T' [palomino mare Seven S Genuine Miss] in Versatility Ranch Horse. We saw the first competition in Fort Worth and knew we had a mare that was perfect for the class because she is really good at a lot of things, but she's not just great at any one thing."

Littlefield says these events fit well with the Stuart Ranch doctrine. "The outstanding element about the Versatility Ranch Horse shows for us is that this ranch has never gotten away from the idea

Miss T, whose registered name is Seven S Genuine Miss (Genuine Doc X Seven S Margarita) is a repeat VRH champion representing the Stuart Ranch of Waurika, Oklahoma, with Chris Littlefield in the saddle. Here the duo circles a calf during the working ranch class in 2002 at the R. A. Brown Ranch in Throckmorton, Texas.

that we are trying to breed the great all-around horse. We are not trying to breed horses that specialize toward reining, cutting, or jumping. We need a horse that we can go do everything on to do ranch work. We want them to be smooth traveling because we'll be riding them all day. They have to have the temperament to be roped off of and to drag a calf. We breed them to have good feet under them for the rough terrain here. The idea of the VRH confirms the goal behind our breeding program."

Breeding Your Own Horse

If you choose to raise your own Quarter Horses for competition, do not attempt to rush the process. "Being effective and efficient in the horse business is a long-term venture," Chris Littlefield of Stuart Ranch says. "Efficient is getting the maximum results in a timely manner. A timely manner in the breeding/training/showing business is five years. If you have a proven individual, a stud, and you breed it to a mare, you don't really know what kind of horses you're getting until five years down the road when you've started that colt and seen what he's capable of getting done on the ranch."

Not all horses with talent pass those outstanding characteristics on to their progeny. In 1973, Secretariat became the first horse to win the Triple Crown in twenty-five years. Remarkably, he didn't just win; he flat outran the other horses, finishing thirty-one lengths ahead of any other entry. Ironically, Secretariat was sold for more than $6 million to a breeding syndicate to cover estate taxes left by his owner's death. The syndicate would take control of the stallion when his racing days ended. In stud, Secretariat sired less than a handful of winners. There was 1986

Horse of the Year Lady's Secret and 1988 Preakness and Belmont winner Risen Star. But none of his offspring came close to matching the standard he set.

On the flip side of the coin, some otherwise standard horses produce outstanding offspring. For example, Seven S Zanaday of the Stuart Ranch has earned AQHA points in seven events and is a solid heading horse. "Where he stands out is as a breeding horse," Littlefield says. "His colts are performing better than he ever did. Again, it takes years to discover how your horse program is shaping up. Anyone out there interested in breeding horses should know that it requires more input than exposing a mare to a stallion."

It will take approximately five years to get this young foal through enough training to know its temperament, athletic ability, and performance potential. Then its breeder will know more about the cross made between sire and dam.

However, a quality horse doesn't have to be home raised. If you want to purchase a horse, Littlefield provides some criteria that are important to him. "The number one thing that I look for in any horse is structural correctness," he continues. "Then I look for adequate muscling. I don't want a horse too big or too small. Some people say our horses are too big to work a cow. But if they are too small, they aren't strong enough to carry a rider all day. It's a balance that you find from years of experience. We like genetics that offer some cow and some performance bloodlines. It doesn't scare me at all to have an outcross bloodline that isn't very well known. If he's a good horse, I'll give it a try. I believe in good horses."

For the Stuart Ranch, good mares can often be evidenced by their progeny. "We like a mare that has produced and her daughters are producing," general manager Terry Stuart Forst says. "She will have her offspring as evidence to the strength of her own pedigree. Being a performer is valuable, but to us, it's more important to have a producer. If she can perform too, that's great, but we want to know that she can help grow our horse program with her breeding ability."

It doesn't scare me at all to have an outcross bloodline that isn't very well known. If he's a good horse, I'll give it a try. I believe in good horses.—*Chris Littlefield, Stuart Ranch*

While Craig Haythorn, owner of the Haythorn Land and Cattle Company in Arthur, Nebraska, looks for conformation also, he incorporates a few other guidelines. "I prefer gelding and studs to mares because they seem to stay focused better," Haythorn says. "Athleticism, bloodlines, age, and temperament all are major factors in choosing which horses we use to work and show."

Bill Smith of Espuela Land and Cattle Company near Spur, Texas, agrees with Haythorn about gender preferences. "I think a gelding is a lot easier to be around," he says. "I have ridden a couple

Craig Haythorn competed on two studs at the ranch horse competition of the Western Heritage Classic in May 2004. This turn on the fence becomes a thing of beauty when executed by 1999 gray stallion PG Shogun (Playgun X Miss Sho Bunny).

Bill Smith considers natural rate to be the horse's ability to stay in a gait on a slack rein until asked for a change by the rider. During the 2004 Western Heritage Classic, Smith prepares to rope while gray gelding Tens Quick (Ten O Sea X Quick Gray Chick) rates the calf.

of my studs in shows and spent a lot of time in the last few years riding them when I could have made two or three more geldings. But I like to get the studs out and show them."

Smith says that letting the public witness how his studs handle helps him sell the foals he raises with the thirty broodmares he keeps each year. Smith also likes his horses to show rate and balance. "It seems you can make one go and whoa so much easier when they have the characteristic of natural rate," Smith says. "I think the balance is important because you do a lot of loping in these events and you need one that naturally lopes well."

Trainer Kim Lindsey added that she has found "reject" reining horses work well in the VRH classes. "They seem to have all the basics of training already done," she says. "If you have to buy a horse and have access to a trainer who might have a reining prospect that didn't quite work, consider that possibility. Most reining horses are cow-bred, which is beneficial for the cow events in VRH. In my experience, cutting horses have lots of movement about them, but consistently they aren't as well-trained on the basics.

"When I purchase a horse, I look for one with the training basics that is super gentle," Lindsey continues. "My intention is to take these horses to shows, expose them to a multitude of events to add the finishing touches, and then sell them. And, I get to have a lot of fun doing it. First, I want a horse that is safe, so I can feel comfortable that I'm selling a solid horse that won't hurt whoever buys it. Second, I want a pretty horse. I like one that is nicely put together and stands out from the crowd. Third, I look at the pedigree for solid bloodlines."

Age of the horse should be a determining factor for exhibitors. Traveling to shows and training for shows can be physically challenging for older animals, but it can be mind blowing for younger horses that haven't established a high confidence level. A common piece of advice throughout the horse industry is to remember that green and green do not match. This translated means that a green horse and green rider are not a good match. If you are inexperienced, find a solid, well-trained horse that can help guide you through the newness of the show ring. If you are an experienced horseperson, you have a little more room to experiment with horses of various ages and training levels.

In January 2004, Kansas rancher Bill James was prepared to compete at the National Western Stock Show in Denver on his sorrel stud Three Jay Colonel. The week of the event, a close friend of James's died and he needed to stay home to pay his respects. Enter James's helpful horseman and grandson, Jamie Stover, to head to Denver and show the horse. The only challenge facing the duo was that Jamie had never competed in the VRH classes. His time horseback was most often spent roping. By day two, Stover and Three Jay Colonel were making waves at the show. "What did I do?" asked

As a first-time versatility contestant, Kansas cowboy Jamie Stover worked with his grandfather's sorrel stallion Three Jay Colonel (Colonel Hotrodder X Cuatro Blanco) to win the VRH competition at the 2004 National Western Stock Show in Denver.

Stover between classes. "Well, I just read the rule book and tried to memorize the patterns. I knew if I didn't guide my horse wrong, he would do what he can do and maybe we could end up in a respectable placing." Stover's "maybe" became "certainly" when he won the double-judged show under judge Dick Pieper of Marietta, Oklahoma, placing first in working ranch horse and ranch conformation. The new team finished second under judge Tom McBeath of Union, Missouri. "He's good at showing his versatility," Stover says of Three Jay Colonel. "Now that I've had him to lead me through it, I think I might try to compete more on one of my own horses." Three Jay Colonel provided a good example of a solid horse teaching a rider a new way to enjoy his time in the saddle.

Double Judged/Double Point Status

Major livestock shows or state fairs that have two judges judging the same class independently of each other at one show, resulting in two sets of points.
—*From the showing glossary of www.aqha.com*

The age of the horse is not as important as the temperament of the horse to Bill Smith. "The shows are encouraging people to start their horses younger," Smith says. "We don't push them. We let a horse finish his two-year-old year not doing much, but we will show him through his five-year-old year as a junior horse. A lot of people from this area used to think that a six- or seven-year-old horse hadn't been ridden enough to be solid because everyone waited longer to start their horses.

"Regardless of the age, I like a horse that is quiet," he explains. "I guess everybody does. I want him to be light and responsive. Let me say that there is a difference between being quiet and being not trained and not responsive to what you are asking him to do." Smith described that this difference should be made apparent with a simple, quick ride

Experienced trainer Joe Wolter, of Aspermont, Texas, ropes a calf off of four-year-old red roan stallion Strawberry Boon (Peptoboonsmal X Shinys Star) at the 2004 Ranch Horse Association of America National Finals in Abilene, Texas.

around the arena, but with some horses it requires several saddles before you can know how your horse responds.

Stuart Ranch also values a good disposition in each of its horses, sometimes even above proven bloodlines. As Littlefield explained, bloodlines are not a sure-fire way to pick a solid horse with bred-in cow sense. Being around the horse in both stressful and stress-free situations can let you have some insight to disposition.

"We put a lot of emphasis on disposition with our horses," says Terry Stuart Forst, general manager of Stuart Ranch. "That's been a big issue in growing the horse-related aspect of our business. All of our stallions have been tremendously well-dispositioned horses. We got into a horse that was not. He was all right, but his colts weren't well dispositioned. So we got rid of him and his colts. There is no remnant of that horse in this operation and our output is better because of that decision."

The Haythorn Ranch manages its horse program with the philosophy of breeding and raising all of its own horses except for the studs it has purchased to complement the characteristics of its broodmare remuda. "We have had the opportunity to purchase PG Shogun and Gunnin To Play from Dick Pieper and Texas Stray from Jim Mapes," Haythorn says. Haythorn showed both of the Pieper-purchased studs at the Ranch Horse Association of America National Finals in Abilene, Texas, on May 8, 2004. It was a busy weekend. In the junior class (foaled 1999 or younger), which started with fifteen horses in the first round, PG Shogun took Top Junior Horse honors and Gunnin To Play took fourth place. Both horses competed in the open class as well and PG Shogun finished third. In the Western Heritage Classic competition PG Shogun was the Top Senior Horse, ridden by Haythorn. Haythorn also rode the Top Junior Horse, Gunnin To Play.

Looking at the two studs, the family resemblance is obvious. PG Shogun, "Gunner," is a 1999 gray stallion by Playgun and out of Miss Sho Bunny. He is owned by F&H Horses, a partnership between Haythorn and Mark Freeman. Gunnin To Play is a 1999 gray stallion by Playgun and out of Little Santana Pep. Gunnin To Play is also owned by F&H Horses.

Remuda
Group of working horses bred for the ranch specifically to work and pen cattle.
—*American Quarter Horse Journal*

The family resemblance between these two Haythorn Land and Cattle Company studs is obvious in their coloring and their movements. Above, Gunnin To Play and Haythorn prepare to rope a calf, and below, PG Shogun turns a cow on a fence.

FOR SALE

Where can you find a ranch horse to purchase? Head to a quality ranch horse sale. Ask around at the veterinarians' offices and trainers' barns to find out who consistently conducts well-managed sales with quality horses. Keep your eye on sale ads in the *American Quarter Horse Journal* and other reputable publications.

According to Littlefield, "Nowadays, there are several top-quality sales. People are becoming more adapted to buying a horse from a sale. In the past the only reason a person might take a horse to a sale was to get rid of it. Now you can feel good about paying a decent price for a horse that is backed by a solid ranch."

Do your research on what ages and types of horses are being offered before you travel hundreds of miles. Contact the people running the sale and request a catalog or go online and see what you can learn before you make a trip and come home disappointed. Many sales, such as the Van Norman and Friends Production Sale in Elko, Nevada, are annual events with horses representing an average of eight different ranches. The longevity of this sale speaks to the high quality of horses they provide, their sales management skills, and the strength of the ranch horse market.

The Best of the Remuda and the Return to the Remuda Sales bring together the ranches that have received AQHA's Best of the Remudas award, the highest honor for Quarter Horse breeders. Past honorees include the Bar B Ranch of Beaver, Oklahoma; The Four Sixes of Guthrie, Texas; R. A. Brown Ranch of Throckmorton, Texas; Stuart Ranch of Waurika, Oklahoma; and the Haythorn Land and Cattle Company of Arthur, Nebraska. Other qualifying ranches are the Pitchfork Land and Cattle Company of Guthrie, Texas; CS Cattle Company of Springer, New Mexico; Bogle Ltd. of Dexter, New Mexico; Waggoner Ranch of Vernon, Texas; Van Norman Ranches of Tuscarora, Nevada; W. H. Green Cattle Company

AQHA Best of the Remuda Sales offer horses consigned by some of the top ranches in the American Quarter Horse industry. Rob Brown of R. A. Brown Ranch in Throckmorton, Texas, right, talks with an attendee before the sale.

of Albany, Texas; Lacey Livestock Company of Paso Robles, California; and Douglas Lake Cattle Company of British Columbia, Canada. The sales are hosted in alternate years by one of the award-winning ranches.

The demand for ranch horses was strong at the 2005 AQHA Best of the Remuda Sale in Fort Worth, Texas. The top seller, Roosters

At many of the reputable sales, consigned horses are put through the paces by a ranch employee to show their natural cow ability, ability to set up a roper, and general demeanor.

Senorita, was consigned by the W. T. Waggoner Estate. The 2002 buckskin filly by Gallo Del Cielo and out of The Genuine Senorita by Genuine As Diamonds brought $33,000. Other high-dollar horses included Ginnin Whiskey, a 2002 brown stallion by Paddys Irish Whiskey and out of Happy Ginnin by Tanquery Gin. Consigned by The Four Sixes Ranch, the stallion brought $20,500. The Pitchfork Land and Cattle Company consigned Pay Twenty Nine, a 1997 gray gelding, which also sold for $20,500. Pay Twenty Nine is by Pay Forty Four and out of Ms Fork Twenty Nine by Mr Gray Fork. Rank Of Colonel, a 1996 brown gelding by Docen Colonel and out of Robin Taris Candi by Robin Tari, brought $15,700 and was consigned by Bogle Ltd. Bogle Ltd. also consigned Four Lakes Lady 011, a 1999 sorrel mare by Docen Colonel and out of Sweet Pepo Scooter by Peppy Motorscooter, who brought $14,000. The 2005 AQHA Best of the Remuda Sale consigned 190 horses. Of these, 79 head sold for a total of $353,850, making the average sale price $4,479.

Prices were also steady during the 2005 Invitational Ranch Horse Show and Sale. Each of the ranches is invited to bring one accomplished ranch horse to represent its brand. The horses compete in a detailed competition that includes roping cattle, cutting, and sorting. Buyers watch the horses perform before the sale begins. Rounsaville Cattle Company of Olney, Texas, provided the 2005 top-selling horse, Leana Get Your Gun. The 1998 sorrel gelding by Playgun and out of My May Olena by Doc O'Lena brought $44,000.

The winner of the ranch horse competition was Dried Out Bill by Bill Cogdell and out of Dun Dryed by The Dry Hand. "Coop," a 1999 chestnut gelding, was consigned by Tongue River Ranch of Dumont, Texas. Coop was started by cowboy Stoney Jones, who rode the gelding in several ranch rodeos. Jones is known in the ranch horse industry for having quiet hands that bring the best out of any horse he rides. The gelding sold for $20,500.

As an example of places to locate a horse, a quick scan of the Internet can come up with thousands of options. Most of the Best of the Remuda-honored ranches have established Web sites with their history, breeding programs, horses for sale, and other interesting tidbits of information. (For Web site addresses, refer to the appendix.)

The Open Box Rafter Ranch in South Dakota is run by fourth-generation cattle ranchers and horse breeders Jim and Joni Hunt. In 2004, they stood eleven studs and each one is detailed on their Web site, www.RafterRanch.com. The operation is one of many that use www.HorseAuctions.com and www.StallionAlley.com to list the horses they have for sale during their annual production sale.

Tim and Vicky Ettleman of Longmont, Colorado, use their Web site at www.EttlemanRanch.com or www.EttlemanQuarterHorses.com to promote their business. Visitors can learn more about the Ettlemans' horse operation, view horses for sale on the sale corral page, and link to organizations and associations promoting the Western stock horse. When appropriate, Ettleman has included photos and three-generation pedigrees for the horses discussed. On the bottom of each page, contact information is provided.

To find a professional horse trainer who can guide you to horses that are well bred and well trained, visit www.4ahorse.com and look up a professional, AQHA-approved trainer in your area and discipline.

BE YOUR OWN ADVERTISING FIRM

Selecting the best horse to show can be beneficial to your operation beyond the ribbons and AQHA points. The ranchers interviewed for this book were unanimous in the opinion that the VRH competitions provide an outlet to show their "wares" to an interested market.

Martin Black showed Blue Duck, top, and Play Lika Hickory (Doc's Hickory X Freckles Playmate), below, in Texas, branching out to markets other than his native Homedale, Idaho.

Haythorn also recognizes the value of advertising from the show ring. "Showing horses has a tremendous impact on our operation," Haythorn says. "Anytime you can be seen or win something in the public eye, it is a bonus. In your attempt to keep in the limelight of whatever you are doing, exposure is the greatest advertising tool there is."

Stuart Ranch agrees.

"It's a good deal to go show because we have a breeding program and training program," Littlefield says. "The VRH allows us to advertise our horses. If you are a small-time breeder, it is a nice way to introduce your horses to the public and maybe earn some AQHA points, which will go right on their record and hopefully increase their market value. You never know where you are going to tap into a market. Showing a stud or mare can spark some interest from another competitor, a member of show staff, like the judge or someone in the crowd."

Original AQHA Versatility Ranch Horse Task Force member and competitor Bob Moorhouse of the Pitchfork Land and Cattle Company summarizes, "The Versatility Ranch Horse competition provides something for everyone. You get to show your horse, learn what your horse is capable of doing, and enjoy yourself too. Then because you've got a set standard, you are given a bar to measure yourself by and it makes you want to go home and work on the horse's weaknesses to be stronger in the next competition."

Smith, who has seen the organized competition of ranch horses develop from inception, feels that the horses have improved, but so have the people showing the horses.

"I think the Versatility Ranch Horse and RHAA have helped people in this part of the country learn horsemanship," Smith says. "They are starting to really learn what makes a horse tick. We are fortunate that we have the opportunity and land to ride a horse lots of miles, although you can get a quiet horse dulled out really quick that way. But if we are headed to a show, I can get on and ride the horse through a couple of maneuvers, change his mind-set, and have him sharpened up. We didn't have that opportunity before these type events came around."

Working with these ideas and your own requirements for finding the right Quarter Horse for you will give you a solid starting point in your quest to become a successful VRH competitor. To learn more about the sport, attend several VRH competitions hosted by different groups, if possible. Watch the classes closely and evaluate the horses that represent each ranch. After a few shows, you will notice that you are consistently drawn to a certain type of horse, probably owned by the same ranch. It might be a horse that has lots of cow ability or a horse that is quite laid-back. As your exposure creates the full picture of the type of horse that interests you, research the bloodlines of that horse and talk to a ranch representative about its foal crops, sales, and training programs. Once you have collected the information you want, go find your horse.

CHAPTER 3

TRAINING A VERSATILITY RANCH HORSE

THE PROCESS OF TRAINING A HORSE FOR THE VRH COMPETItion is not unlike most other horse training. Give the horse repeated exposure to the situations you want it to tolerate, remain consistent with cues and consequences, and give the process time.

Many of the first successful Versatility Ranch Horses were used on ranches on a daily basis before going to a show. However, a "backyard horse" can compete with these ranch horses if trained correctly to handle the elements involved in the competition.

The mandatory obstacles in trail include opening; passing through and closing a gate; dragging a log in a straight line or around a set pattern; and having the rider dismount, remove the bit completely from the horse's mouth and rebridle, then pick up all four of the horse's feet while the horse remains quiet. Some optional obstacles include crossing a water hazard, being hobbled or ground tied, and crossing a bridge.

As part of the ranch riding class, the horse will need to display three gaits in both directions, maintaining each gait until the next is requested by the judge.

Ranch cutting requires the horse to hold a single cow away from the herd and then pen the separated cow at the other end of the arena.

During the working ranch horse class, the exhibitors are required to circle, perform lead changes, complete a 360-degree turn, and

execute a roll-back. They also are expected to box the cow at one end of the arena, take the cow down the fence, and turn it both directions. The rider should then rope the cow.

OVERALL APPROACH

Some ranchers will handle their horses from birth to imprint them with the human touch and smell. Others leave them in the pasture until their second or third year. Each operation has a different program and you should look into different options. Take time to evaluate your horse's needs as well before you decide what tactics will work for your situation. Flexibility in the training process will enable you to grow as a trainer by learning to read each horse and allow for individuality to emerge.

The Espuela Example

"We brand our foals in July when they are two to three months old," Bill Smith of the Espuela Land and Cattle Company says. "Then they aren't handled again until the winter or fall when they are weaned. Colts are gentler now than they have been because most ranchers keep them around the pen and feed them, whereas they used to grow up entirely in the pasture. We will begin to ride them around the first

Each July, Bill Smith and friends gather and brand his foal crop. Following the branding, the foals are returned to the pasture with their mothers until they are weaned in the winter.

year to bring up cattle and drag a few calves on them. We get in the chute and rope some, but mainly we start our young horses out dragging calves when we brand. Around their three-year-old year, we work on getting them bending and guiding. We don't expect a whole lot from them. We let them train themselves."

Smith stands behind the idea that a horse needs to learn to interact with horses and humans. A horse learns everything from other horses—from running and playing, to hierarchy, to responding to humans. "Putting a horse out in the pasture is a good way to let him adjust to the land, weather, and other elements," Smith says. "I don't like the idea of keeping a horse locked up in a stall and then asking him to go deal with all the stuff that can happen in a pasture."

The best way to approach training a horse for versatility competition might be to examine each category to determine the skills required.

RANCH RIDING

The gaits of walk, trot, and lope are simple parts of basic horse training and are required during the ranch riding class. These elements should already be part of your horse's repertoire. According to our sources, the challenge is to display these gaits on ranch horses in a show environment. "Some horses just move beautifully in the pasture," Chris Littlefield of Stuart Ranch says. "Then, you get them in the arena and as a rider you have to steer the horse around a slower entry and you've got strange horses coming up on your horse and it changes the game. I've seen dog-gentle horses be alarmed by another horse and change their lead or drop their gait."

Credit is given to horses that make a smooth transition between gaits, keep the correct lead, and maintain the gait requested until the

Kim Lindsey trains her horses to change gaits by using consistent cues, such as standing in the stirrups to extend the trot.

judge requests a change. A rider must show his horse with only one hand on the reins unless the horse is five years old or younger and is being shown in a snaffle bit or hackamore. Remember that the judge has the discretion to work finalists individually.

The Definition of Gait

AQHA defines gait as a manner of moving the feet: walk, jog, and lope in Western events; walk, trot, and canter in English events. Most people competing in Western events, including the Versatility Ranch Horse, refer to the gaits as walk, trot, and lope, which is technically incorrect, but generally understood and accepted.

To train for the ranch riding class, trainer Kim Lindsey of the Box P Ranch in Jayton, Texas, suggests teaching a horse to change gaits only when it is cued. "I always stand to extend my trot," she says. "Because that's how I do it when we're traveling in the pasture, that's what I do in the practice and show rings. If my horse tries to extend the trot without me asking him to, I rein him in and force him to stay in the regular trot. I have had horses before that just wanted to go. It was work to get them to keep from breaking from a walk to a trot, especially around strange horses. But after time, they didn't try to change speeds until I let them. I'm not saying it was easy. It took a lot of work, but it was worth it when we could stay in the correct gait at a show."

Be reasonable with what you expect of your horse in the ranch riding class. "Set small, realistic goals and build from that foundation," Lindsey advises. "I want to keep my gait, pick up the correct leads, et cetera, on a young horse in a ranch riding class. With a horse that is further along in training, I work on getting his head set, controlling his speeds, getting him to extend the trot when I stand up in the stirrups—the details I consider finishing touches. I want to be consistent in what I'm asking and how I'm asking for it."

Lindsey reminds competitors that the rule book requires AQHA judges to call for an extended trot and an extended lope in at least one direction. "If you aren't prepared for this, it will be immediately obvious to the judge," she says. "These are small parts of the pie that can make a big difference in your overall score."

Head set is also under scrutiny during the ranch riding class. As the horses are moving around the edge of the arena, the rhythmic movement draws the judge's eye to the head set and leg movement. Bill Smith likes his horses to travel with what he calls a natural head set. "We do a lot of head setting, although I'm not as big on a head set as some," Smith explains. "I like the horse to be level-headed. Generally, as long as he doesn't root (get his nose too close to the ground) on you, it's okay with me. I want him flexible at the poll but still responsive when you take hold of him."

Trail

Ranch trail consists of a course with a minimum of six obstacles and is designed to show a horse's ability and willingness to perform tasks that might be asked of him during the course of a normal day's work on the ranch. Mandatory obstacles are opening, passing through and closing a gate; dragging a log; and dismounting, unbridling, rebridling, checking feet, and remounting.

Gate Work

The act of opening a gate, passing through it, and closing it is done daily on ranches. At most VRH events, you'll be dealing with gates that are simple to open on horseback. Show managers are to provide a gate that will not endanger horse or rider.

Opening, passing through, and closing a gate is a common daily activity for horseback cowboys. It is also a mandatory obstacle for AQHA's ranch trail class, as seen here with Buster Reed and The Next Doc (Doc The Dock X Holly Sugar Lynx). The 1998 sorrel gelding owned by Mill Iron Horse and Cattle Company of Hamlin, Texas, is not bothered by the banner hanging on the gate.

Lindsey suggests preparing by bringing your horse parallel to your practice gate. If you need to get closer to the gate, side pass a step or two until you are in place. Next, you can place your reins in the hand opposite the gate. Lean over to open the gate. Navigate through the open gate. Be aware of your horse moving through the gate. Do not let the gate hit the horse in the hindquarters. Using leg and reining aids, move your horse parallel to the gate again until you are situated to close the gate.

AQHA rules state that the rein hand may be changed to work the gate without penalty if the change is made prior to and after the gate has been worked.

It is advisable not to take your hand off of the gate until it is latched to prevent it from swinging either away from your horse or into your horse during judging. Take your time practicing and performing this so that you and your horse are ready to handle any challenges that might occur.

Pulling a Log

"It may seem too simple, but tie a rope to a log and drag it," Littlefield says. "Of course, you'll want to get your horse used to the log, so you might move it into the dry lot or wherever you train for a few days. This allows your horse to see it, smell it, and know that the log is not a threat." Most ranch horses have been asked to drag calves to a branding fire and are not unfamiliar with moving a weight. If your horse is not accustomed to pulling, it is certainly a skill that can be taught.

"Start by moving the log short distances and work up to a figure-eight pattern," advises Littlefield. The horse should be able to approach the log at any point without balking. During the ranch trail portion of a show, a five-point penalty is assessed for the first refusal, balk, or attempt to evade an obstacle by moving more than two

During the ranch trail class, an exhibitor can expect to pull a log behind his horse with a rope. George Self steers gray gelding Ima Eddie Hancock around the brush during a ranch trail class at The Four Sixes in Guthrie, Texas. Ima Eddie Hancock is owned by the R. A. Brown Ranch of Throckmorton, Texas.

strides from it. A second refusal will equal an additional five-point penalty. Also, the rope should be dallied around the saddle horn for this obstacle. Never tie the rope hard and fast to your saddle.

Dismounting, Bridle Work, Foot Examination, and Remounting

There are no tricks to teaching a horse to trust its rider and that is made evident by the trail element of dismounting, removing the bridle, examining the feet, and remounting. To practice, Bill Smith says you should bring your horse to a stop while riding in an enclosed space and sit for a moment or two. "Then, dismount and approach the horse's head," Smith says. "I usually drop the reins because my horses ground tie, but this isn't written in as part of the program. I make sure I'm always relaxed because horses can tell if you aren't and they'll let everyone else know it too. So, I unbridle the horse, shake the headstall once or twice just to let everything fall back into place, and rebridle. I might pick up the reins and drop them again to reiterate to my horse that he's staying right where he is.

"Then I approach the feet. I run my hand down the horse's side from the withers to the lower part of the pastern, apply a little pressure, and let the horse pick up his hoof. I am bent at this point and cradle the hoof in my hand to view the sole. Repeat this technique with the other front leg. The back legs are about the same, but you will start with your hand on the horse's hip to let him know you've moved to his hind end. Run your hand down and usually when you get just under the hock, the horse will give you his foot.

"After you've examined all four feet, you can remount," Smith continues. "Let your reins have some slack and make sure they are even before you get back on. Once you do, get settled in the saddle before you ride forward."

A gentle horse will allow you to pick up all four feet with the proper approach. This is beneficial for hoof care or administering medical attention, and it is a training tactic that farriers greatly appreciate. Smith says you never want to attempt to force the horse to give you its foot because it's hard for any two-hundred-pound human to manhandle a twelve-hundred-pound horse. During practice, be patient and allow the horse to offer the foot to you.

Optional Trail Obstacles

Any three of the following eight obstacles could be part of a ranch trail course within the Versatility Ranch Horse event. Show managers may decide to incorporate a water hazard, bridge, or crossing obstacle. The rider might be asked to hobble or ground tie the horse; put on and remove a rain slicker; remove, carry, and replace an item; ride over four or more logs; or rope a stationary steer.

One optional ranch trail obstacle is roping a stationary steer as performed by Katherine Lyons, of Wiggins, Colorado, on bay mare Sliks Sweet Tart at a Woodward, Oklahoma, event.

Hobble or Ground Tie

Ground tie

A horse that ground ties will stand as if tied when the reins are dropped on the ground.

—*Chris Littlefield, Stuart Ranch*

Although it is not required, ground tying is often used by exhibitors during the dismounting/unbridling/foot examination/remounting portion of the ranch trail class. A horse that will ground tie allows the rider to have both hands completely unencumbered while examining the horse's feet.

A horse that will ground tie makes it convenient for cowboys to dismount and have both hands free for various tasks around the ranch.

To train a horse to ground tie, Bill Smith suggests starting the process when you dismount and continue to do it as often as possible. "I start at the barn or the pen and ride the horse to a stop," he says. "Then I throw a rein down and just sit there. Then I get off of him and lay the other one down. After a month of doing this daily, you might not be able to get very far from him, but gradually you teach him.

"I make sure to lay those reins out in front of him where he actually sees them and knows that he is loose," Smith continues. "I don't try to disguise it. When you leave, don't ever lead him off. Get back on and ride him off. Lots of people are teaching their horses to come to them in the round pen/groundwork training, but that is confusing when you start teaching ground tying and the horse thinks it is supposed to follow you. As you start creating a foundation for your horse, try to think ahead about any conflicts you might be starting."

What do you do when your horse starts to follow? Smith says to go back to him and say whoa.

Crossing a Bridge

Most competitors don't have the opportunity to cross a bridge on a daily basis, but many have created the obstacle at home to help their horses become familiar with the task. The goal of this obstacle is to show that your horse is willing to be ridden across a change in terrain.

Keep Obstacles from Being Obstacles

"It amazes me that AQHA includes a list of mandatory obstacles for the trail class, but some people show up and you can tell their horses have never seen some of these obstacles," Lindsey says. "Set up some obstacles or use the terrain around you to get your horse comfortable with these challenges. I think it's a waste of money to show up and not be on a horse with enough handle to let you open a gate from the saddle or cross a bridge."

Kim Lindsey sets up an inexpensive, mobile jump made of concrete blocks and PVC pipe to prepare her horses for ranch trail class obstacles. She emphasizes that this device is easy for one person to adjust and rearrange.

CONFORMATION

The purpose of the class is stated in the AQHA Official Handbook of Rules and Regulations as: to preserve American Quarter Horse type by selecting well-mannered individuals in the order of their resemblance to the breed ideal and that are the most positive combination of balance, structural correctness and movement with appropriate breed and sex characteristics and adequate muscling.

To that purpose, you will need to have your horse set up and standing still after trotting a short distance. Teaching a horse to stand still while waiting for a judge to complete his examination isn't as easy as you might think. However, repetition can help you prepare to enter the ring. Take ten to fifteen minutes to halter your horse after you unsaddle and stand him up while a friend walks around the horse at all angles. You should also practice jogging beside your trotting horse. Done often enough, this will help acclimate your horse to the new experience.

At one show, Lindsey attempted to school on her horse directly prior to the conformation class. "I had this old slowpoke horse that doesn't lead well and basically wants you to drag him," she says. "So I was going to tune him up before we entered the ring, but he showed me. We got in there and he balked like a mule. He would not take a step. What could I do? I just had to laugh it off and say, 'Not today.' He taught me a lesson about not being prepared. I went home and we worked on this simple task to keep that from happening again."

During the 2004 National Western VRH conformation class in Denver, 2003 AQHA president Steve Stevens of Houston, Texas, looked over the horses, took the microphone, and said to the audience and exhibitors, "This demonstrates the versatility of the Quarter Horse breed. You have seen in the other classes what these horses are used for. This class shows that a horse can have great conformation and still be ridden."

Many exhibitors stress over the presentation of their horses in the conformation class. It is not expected that the ranch horse entries be fitted out like AQHA World Show Halter entries. However, the show format will help you determine if you have time to rinse your horse off before going into the conformation class. "If you have time, say for example, one of the cattle classes is before conformation and you are at the first of the rotation, try to rinse off your horse before going into conformation," Lindsey advises. "This will knock off the sweat marks from the saddle and provide a cleaner view for the judge. If you don't have time for a rinse, be sure to brush the horse off."

The Cattle Classes—Working Ranch Horse and Ranch Cutting

Once you get a horse to the point where the basics of riding are second nature, it's time to begin giving it something to think about. For most ranch horses, that something is cattle.

"To me, the most extensive element of training would be the cow work," Haythorn says. "It takes so long to perfect it and you have so many uncontrollable variables. The rest of what you will be

Cattle classes are often the most challenging for exhibitors and horses because of the uncontrollable variable of the cow, yet exhibitors also say they enjoy the challenge.

training for is rather cut and dried . . . like the stops, spins, figure eights, and lead changes."

Every trainer might have a different game plan, but we've taken a decent mix of the training philosophies our sources discussed to give you more than one horse trainer's opinion. First, let's tackle the idea of introducing your horse to cattle.

"Midway in their two-year-old year or early in their third year is when I put most of my horses on cattle," Littlefield says. "That's a little later in the horse's development than some trainers, but it is what works for me. When I start them on cattle, most of it is done in an arena because the controlled environment is safer for everyone involved. If you start this lesson in the pasture and a cow breaks away, you'll end up running your horse too early to get around the cow. That won't help teach the horse to watch a cow. That will only teach the horse to go fast."

A horse that can rate a cow shows well in the cattle classes of the Versatility Ranch Horse competitions. Holly Major, of Flower, Colorado, rates this black baldy on her 1997 bay stallion RPM Mr Stylish.

Beyond your horse's ability to handle the cow work is mastering your own ability to read cattle. Smith sees this aspect from both the competitor's and judge's vantage points.

New Venue, New Horse

Don't be too critical of a horse if you've only seen it work in one environment. Horses that perform well but not exceptionally in the pasture might show better on the soft dirt of the arena. Before you eliminate a horse from the show ring, give it a chance to prove its ability in the show environment.

"You can practice every step of the classes, but when you get to town, you have everybody watching, and different cattle," Smith says. "That is a big part of the versatility class and in RHAA, too. You have to be able to read cattle and to judge how the cow you draw is going to work. From boxing the cow in working ranch horse to roping, I see a lot of people who work their calves for so long that when it is time to rope, the calf doesn't have any wind left. You have to learn to gauge different calves to find their tolerance level so that you have enough cow to show off your horse."

As a judge at many of the ranch-horse-based events, Smith says too many exhibitors come into the arena, misuse their cow, and then want another one. He feels the exhibitors should know how to read a cow and not zap all its energy before the competition is finished.

Rate a cow

When you first start a colt, you want him to be able to walk, trot, and lope on a reasonably slack rein. That will tell you if he'll be able to rate a cow or not. To me, it is being able to put the horse in a slow trot

---

behind a cow and he'll maintain a consistent speed
until you ask him to change speeds.
—*Bill Smith, Espuela Land and Cattle Company*

"Rate is pretty much bred into one," Haythorn says. "He either has it or you can help it out a little, but a horse that naturally rates is easier to train than a horse that doesn't rate. It is easier to push than pull."

Smith uses rating a cow to disguise the fact that he's teaching his horse lead changes simultaneously. "I use my rating to teach lead changes and my lead changes to put the horse in the right spot to rate," Smith says. "I think most everybody does it this way. I put in a lot of time while we are tracking cattle from one pasture to the next. I will get on the outside of the cattle and keep the horse on the back of a particular calf. Going left, I will stay on his right hip and then when the calf changes direction, I will change leads and move to the left of his hip. This allows me to get in the control of lead changes while the horse has his mind on the calf. Then his natural balance will teach him in time that he is changing directions so he will change leads."

It might seem appropriate to lope lots of hard, fast circles with flying lead changes to prep your horse for the lead changes in the VRH events, but horses will soon despise loping in circles. "I know people start loping circles immediately after they get on their horse," Smith continues. "If they only have an arena, maybe that's necessary. But I might not lope circles on a colt for six or eight months. I want to teach him to go somewhere. We get a lot of rate that way. Our cattle have been handled and are reasonably gentle, so we get to ride a lot of good slow miles. If you can't do that, think about it as making him where he will walk, trot, lope, and rate himself before you do a lot of cattle handling on him."

Working Ranch Horse

The reining patterns incorporate circles loped in both directions with lead changes transitioning the horse and rider from one direction to

Martin Black, of Homedale, Idaho, executes a near-textbook stop aboard "Blue Duck" at the 2004 RHAA National Finals. The horse is tucking his hind end, paddling his front feet, and keeping his head in a natural, balanced position.

the next. The patterns also include roll-backs, stops, spins, and speed control. All of these maneuvers should be done under the rider's light hand with minimal visual cues. The cow work requires the exhibitors to box the cow at one end of the arena, then rate the cow against one side of the arena, and then turn the cow on the fence. Exhibitors should turn the cow both directions on the fence. Roping involves roping the cow and stopping it, without throwing the cow on the ground or dragging the animal. The entire class is completed under a six-minute time limit.

Lead Changes

Left Lead

The horse's left foreleg extends during a lope or canter. Right Lead—The horse's right foreleg extends during a lope or canter. A lead change occurs when the horse switches from extending one foreleg to extending the other.

—*Charlie Hemphill, AQHA*

"Lead changes are the hardest part for a lot of cowboys to get down for the arena," Smith says. "I think horses do it naturally when you are out in the pasture, but without the tree or bush to use as a reason to change leads, we sometimes have trouble getting the horse to react accurately to our cues.

"To take off riding a horse, anywhere, I like to get him to fall into a lead," he continues. "If I am going in the left lead, I will squeeze him with my right leg and lift my left rein. I think that lifts his left shoulder. Where other people might bend him to the right, I use leg pressure. Now, we might go six months without worrying about a lead change, but at about six months to a year I like to have a horse where I can ask for a specific lead departure either way."

If you have a hard time determining if your horse is in the correct lead or not, do not give up. "I've been riding horses since I was a young child," Lindsey says, who now has a young child of her own. "Only in the last ten years could I tell what lead my horse was in without looking. You don't have to be perfect to go into a show ring and be judged. What you have to be is willing to learn."

When performing lead changes, contestants will score better if changes can be made with minimal visual cues. To Haythorn this is accomplished by training reliably and riding experienced horses. "A good broke horse has very few cues," Haythorn says. "He just responds promptly and properly to whatever he is asked."

You don't have to be perfect to go into a show ring and be judged. What you have to be is willing to learn.
—Kim Lindsey, Box P Ranch

Spins

Spinning is not a move you would see a ranch horse do in a normal day's work. However, it is a move that displays a horse following its head and pivoting on one foot. Smith explains how he gets his ranch horses to spin for the show ring. "I think it takes a really well-trained horse to spin. I ride two-handed a lot, but from day one my goal with every horse is to neck rein. That ability comes in real handy when it is time to spin.

"If I want to turn right, I lay the left rein on his neck and expect him to look right," Smith continues. "You see so many horses being

Spins are a crowd-pleasing move that show the judge a horse will follow its head and pivot on a hind foot. Bill Smith begins spins on his gelding Tens Quick by applying leg pressure and a neck rein to the right side of the horse.

As Bill Smith completes the first spin, notice his left foot is held away from the horse. This gives the horse a "place to go to move away from the leg pressure" Smith is applying on the opposite side.

shown today that counterarc while doing a roll-back. If they want to turn left, they lay the right rein on the horse and the horse immediately looks right. The horses are being trained that way, but I want my horses to make a smooth transition to the neck rein from riding two-handed. I start with the neck reining even before I ride the colt. I will lay the opposite rein on him until he can tell that he needs to move away from that slight pressure. It's the same concept as people using the opposite leg on the horse to move him." Smith lifts the reins slightly to get the horse's attention, so that it lifts its shoulders and begins to arc its neck. Then he neck reins with the opposite rein of the

When Bill Smith changes direction, it is obvious that his horse is responding primarily to the neck reining as both legs are lifted off of the horse's sides.

direction he wants to spin. He nudges the horse with the opposite leg, sits back in the saddle, and begins to spin. Throughout the spin, he encourages the horse to maintain speed by sustaining leg pressure. "If I am working a cow or doing fence work, anytime that I lay a leg on a horse, I want him to get away from my leg," he says. "Not bend, but actually move his feet. I would like to get where we are running down the pen, I squeeze with a leg, and he moves or turns around."

Notice that the horse's hip position is virtually the same, although the front end of the horse has covered ground during the spin.

Turn on a fence

Turning a cow on a fence is a fine art that can earn a horse and rider much respect if done correctly. Knowing your prime area within the arena to execute a turn is one component of a nice turn. "To me, tracking a cow from about fifty yards for a while is the best way to get a horse to hook up with the cow," Smith says. "That's where you start—by getting your horse to watch that cow. Once he's getting hooked each time, you can begin to speed up and slow down. The next step is to pick a set marker, like a fence post, and drive the cow to that marker."

This is not the time to set a horse up to turn on the fence. Your goal is to keep him tracking the cow to the set point. Practice this for months and Smith says you'll be teaching a horse respect for your cues and the cow's reaction. It also will teach a horse to rate.

Once you've got enough control in the horse to try a turn on the fence, take it slowly. Prime your horse on being able to track, then move up the cow's side so the cow can see the horse. You can't stop a cow if you are chasing it. The cow needs to see you in its line of sight.

"I don't stop a horse on the fence," Smith says. "I want him to bend, keep up his motion, and turn with the cow. We know that everything you do on a horse is built on impulsion. So why would you trot this horse by a cow, stop him hard, and kill all your motion? You're asking the horse to do the impossible if you do."

If you turn the cow and you've stopped your horse, your timing will be off because the cow is already ahead of you going down the fence. Then you are chasing the cow again. Timing is critical in cow work. If you get too far behind the cow, you aren't showing your horse well. If you let your horse get too far ahead of the cow, the cow will stop and, again, you aren't showing your horse well. A good cow horse will keep up with the cow, turn it, and be right with the cow to turn it the second time.

This series of four photos shows a nice example of turning a cow on the fence both directions during the working ranch horse class as displayed by Craig Haythorn and **PG Shogun.**

"Fine-tuning a horse to work on the fence would relate to how much cow he has in him," Haythorn says. "It goes back to breeding, but for a horse, the ability to hold a critter will improve every time he does it."

Roping

Roping is a hit-or-miss proposition for any competitor. Lindsey suggests practicing as much as possible. "A lot of the real hands I know would scoff at this, but I'm telling you that if you need practice with the basics of roping, then you should rope the dummy," she says. "I paid my way through college by roping and I still do. I will rope it twenty-five times each set. You don't want to fatigue your arm, but you want to keep your muscle memory." After you have your technique down, then approach the calf in the arena. It will take practice to become consistent at catching the calf.

She suggests finding a rope that you feel comfortable using. "I like to use a poly rope if I'm going to rope something around the neck," she says. "I know you can buy extra soft nylon, but that type is usually made to rope something around the horns. I've roped with both, but would recommend a poly rope because they are easier to handle when roping something around the neck."

In the working ranch horse class, the horse is judged only on its ability to trail, rate, and stop the cow. It is not necessary for the roper to catch to receive a score for the roping portion of the class. However, each exhibitor is allowed two loops. If both are thrown and missed, the exhibitor's run is over and he or she is encouraged to leave the arena so the next exhibitor can begin. If a competitor does not catch the calf, a five-point penalty will be assessed. Please note the total penalty for not catching the calf is a total of five points, not five points per loop attempted. Therefore, if one does catch successfully, it could improve the roping portion of the score.

Kim Lindsey demonstrates her approach to roping a calf.

Exhibitor Lindy Merryman and Jerrys Smokin Too smoothly stop and pull a calf after a successful catch.

Remember, any catch that holds the animal is a legal catch according to AQHA rules. The purpose is to rope the cow and bring it to a stop. Dragging the cow is not allowed.

Ranch Cutting

The goal in the ranch cutting class is to separate a specific numbered cow from the herd and then pen it at the other end of the arena. When you cross the line headed toward the herd, your time will begin and you will scan the herd to locate the bovine with the number you have been given.

Prior to the class, spend time observing the cattle and notice how they respond to the riders who settle the herd and to the competitors who have runs before yours. This vital information can help you determine if the cattle move quickly or are sluggish, and then you can think through how your horse will show best under these conditions.

During the cutting portion, you will have two turnback riders to assist with keeping the cow at the far end of the pen. Once you feel you have displayed your horse's cutting ability, you should motion to the turnback riders to move to the side of the arena opposite the pen. It is required that you push the cow between a cone set twenty to forty feet from the back corner of the pen and the corner of the pen. Then, you should drive the cow into the pen. If the cow isn't penned before the time expires, or if the cow

Bill Smith displays the control his horse "Possum" can have over a cow once the horse-and-rider pair have separated her from the herd. This skill is put into play during the ranch cutting class of Versatility Ranch Horse competition. Possum's registered name is Snippys Crow. He is a 1996 dun gelding by Black Chick Gold and out of Snippy Lena.

returns to the herd, your score will reflect a penalty. To prepare for this event, Bill Smith suggests working without a clock or "set-in-stone" time line.

"I still work a lot of one-on-one with one cow in the pen," Smith says. "Then you progress to working out of the herd. If you start entering the herd too early with a horse, you will lose any confidence you built up in him during the one-on-one work. There are lots of things other than you and your cues that a horse could focus on when you are moving him through a herd to cut out a cow. You want to make sure he's ready for that mentally. I spend most of my time one-on-one and I try not to rush the horse.

"To me, the whole idea is control," he continues. "First is your knowledge about what it takes to control the cow. Second is getting the horse to control the cow. To me a cutting horse is one that can control a cow. The pivots and fast moves look good, but the way I train and the way I look at training is to get the horse into a position to stop that cow. That is my basic philosophy in training a horse. If a horse can get into the cow's view and stop her, he has accomplished his goal."

Practice Makes Perfect

Lindsey encourages beginners to attend any clinics, from horsemanship to riding, in order to further their knowledge base and skill set. "I think the Stock Horse of Texas (SHOT) events are perfect for someone wanting to get into the Versatility Ranch Horse event," she says.

Other than the clinics, Lindsey explains that entering any of the SHOT classes available can help put the polish you want on your horse to compete with the high-caliber competition seen at most VRH events. (See the appendix for more information on SHOT.)

"I'll take my solid horse that I think I might be able to win something on," she says. "And I always take another horse with me that I'm getting started. I head first to a Stock Horse of Texas competition and clinic. I'll enter the young horse in the SHOT Western pleasure class or the reining class to get him familiar with being around other horses, the PA system, even being tied to the trailer while I'm competing on the other horse. Getting him used to all the commotion is essential so that he's not overexposed.

"I want to expose a horse a little bit at a time," she continues. "Competing in that one class can do a lot for him mentally, especially when he's not quite ready to handle all five classes of the Versatility Ranch Horse event, but he's progressed beyond the practice arena."

The SHOT Western pleasure class requires a walk, trot, and lope, a turn, and then the gaits again headed in the other direction. "It's an easy way to introduce the horse to the arena," she says. "I think the SHOT has the greatest pleasure class going because they do one horse at a time. People think that would make the show too long, but I consider that my horse is getting the full attention of the judge during that time, which makes it worthwhile."

Gradually, she adds other classes to the horse's list until she feels they're prepared enough to head into all five of the VRH classes without stressing out the horse. "Competing in one event can help you determine what you need to fine-tune better than having a rough day at a VRH event and maybe not knowing if it was a lead change or handling the cow that made it rough," she explains.

Practice Facilities

It is not necessary to have an expensive, heated, indoor arena with lights and access to ten thousand acres of land to prepare your horse for the VRH competition. Investing in extensive practice facilities is not always a feasible financial option. Lindsey reminds people that she

Kim Lindsey uses dirt roads as straightaways to practice lead changes on the Box P Ranch near Jayton, Texas, where she works. She encourages people who are interested in VRH competition to think creatively about training area options.

is able to compete by fine-tuning her horses in a simple environment. "I think you need a location, preferably a corral, to work cattle. It can be square, oval, or round, but the pen needs to have enough room to maneuver your horse around the cow. If your round pen is big enough to rope in or box a cow in, feel free to use it. Everything else you can do outside. I practice lead changes in the pasture on a straightaway. A dirt road is a good example of a common straightaway. That means we're practicing lead changes without having any stress or any set routine. If you only practice changing leads in the middle of the arena while doing your circles, you'll see that your horse anticipates that pattern. Soon, he'll be doing lead changes before you want or he could get burned out on the routine and balk on you.

"You'll want to make sure you have soft dirt in your pen. Running and stopping on hard dirt can hurt your horse faster than you would think. Be sure to plow it when you can to keep it from firming up and getting too solid."

Lindsey also keeps an area of unfenced flat land near her barns plowed. She uses this area to lope her horses in soft ground and practice jumping and loping over logs. Her goal is to give the horses a change of pace.

Bits on Bits

"We start our colts in a snaffle and then I go back to a hackamore a lot," Bill Smith of Espuela Land and Cattle Company says. "For me, a hackamore teaches patience—for the rider and the horse. When you are having problems with a young horse, the tendency is to get a bigger bit. We probably need to get a smaller bit and slow everything down. A hackamore makes me slow down and actually aid correctly. I have to send him the right signal and not just rely on the bit."

Spookproofing Your Horse

If your horse isn't familiar with an indoor arena, Espuela Land and Cattle Company's Bill Smith advises making a few trips to unfamiliar territory as part of your prep work. Lights, public announcement systems, waving banners, and hoards of people can be a shock to an old ranch horse's system. "It really puts you in a better position to compete if you can spend even just three minutes in the arena letting him look around a little," Smith says. "One time a chalk line became my archenemy. Since then, we put a few chalk lines in the dirt at home and get all our horses used to them being there." He says taking your horse off your property to shows and even to the neighbor's barn can help it get more accustomed to accepting the unfamiliar.

Kim Lindsey uses a burlap sack filled with crushed, empty aluminum cans to "spookproof" her horses. She lets the horse sniff the bag, then she shakes it over and around the horse, even keeping it in her hand once she gets on to ride.

CHAPTER 4

THE COMPETITION

The day of competition brings on intense emotions for many exhibitors. Their heads are filled with unanswered—perhaps unanswerable—questions. Is my horse ready? Will I draw a good cow? What if I forget the patterns? Did I remember all of my gear?

Only you know how to help yourself prepare for the big day. If you need a list of tack, make it. If you need to bring a supportive friend, load her up. But try not to let a lack of preparation be the reason you leave the show disappointed with your performance.

Once you get on the grounds the day of the show, maintain your focus by getting on your horse and warming up. "Get to the arena early, ride around the event site, and let the horse become familiar in the new surroundings," Chris Littlefield of Stuart Ranch advises. "Sometimes banners hanging on the fence can be a wreck waiting to happen. If you get your horse comfortable before the show, you don't have to worry about losing its attention during your run."

Warm-up is a time to prep your horse, not put the finishing touches on unfinished training techniques. "I try to get all my training done at home so that when I get there I can relax and show," Littlefield explains. "If the horse has a weak spot, say changing leads, then I would set him up and run through a few lead changes. This way I can make sure he's listening to my cues. Do not try to retrain your horse in the arena. That isn't the place to school on a horse. One, it looks bad in front of the judges. Two, it will frustrate you. Three, you will confuse your horse."

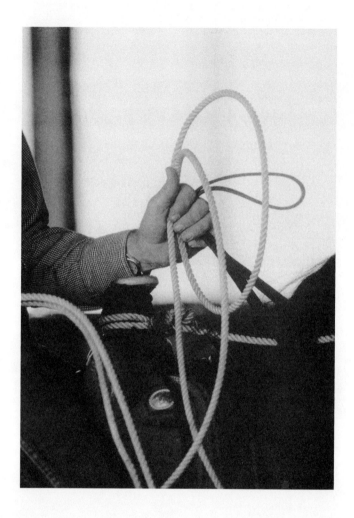

Before most VRH events begin, the show manager, judge, and contestants will meet to make sure all contestants are clear about how the show will be run. According to Box P Ranch's Kim Lindsey, this is not the time to be shy. "Think through your game plan for the day of the show and jot down any questions you might have. If you have a question, ask it. Don't be afraid to clarify something on a pattern

An exhibitor takes time during warm-up to let her horse determine that the bright blue banners at the end of the arena are not scary.

or ask where the judge will be sitting. These things are important to how you show. And you won't have another chance to ask questions, so use your time wisely."

Lindsey believes the score of a prepared exhibitor, who knows the patterns and has a strategy, is higher than the unprepared exhibitor nine out of ten times. Take time to look at the layout of the arena. Go through a visual run while looking at the facilities so you at least have a goal. Note where the cattle will be entering the arena

Two cowboys discuss the show format before a Versatility Ranch Horse competition in Oklahoma.

and identify anything that might pose a problem during your run. See where you will come into the arena. Find a set point that marks the middle of the pen. Loping off center circles or figure eights isn't as pretty as doing your lead changes in the middle of the arena. Lindsey encourages riders to think about showing their horse to the judge specifically.

"For example, during the working ranch horse class, you'll want to try to take your cow down the opposite side from where the judge is sitting to give the best display of your horse's ability," she says. "When you rope, a right-handed person will want to take the cow down the left side of the arena to serve as a boundary. If you're on the right side of the fence, you have to contend with staying far enough away from the fence to keep from interfering with your loop." Try to set up the cow so that the judge does not have to lean over the rail to watch your horse perform.

Bill Smith, of Spur, Texas, makes sure his calf is set up before he begins roping in order to best show his horse's ability. Smith is riding Tens Quick.

Proper Paperwork Is a Plus

Having the proper paperwork on hand as you head to the competition is vital to being admitted on the grounds. Use this list as a reference for where to begin.

- AQHA registration papers
- Coggins papers
- Copies of any correspondence with event staff (i.e., receipt of entry fees)
- Health papers (at larger shows to access grounds)

"I have found the easiest thing to do is to put together a notebook," Kim Lindsey, of Box P Ranch, says. "I make copies of all the cards for the different associations I belong to. That sheet goes first. Then, I have my horse papers in a plastic sheet with his Coggins papers on the back side. It's handy to have that set up with each horse. Plus, if you sell a horse, you can remove his information from the plastic sleeve and reuse it for another horse."

Lindsey makes photocopies of each entry she submits with the date she entered the event, the check number, and the date the check was written. That small effort makes any paperwork confusion at a show easier to sort out.

ABIDE BY THE RULES

"If you don't know the rules of the competition, don't even bother showing up," Lindsey suggests. "You might as well throw your entry money out the window on the way to the show if you don't know the rules. I can tell you from experience. I went to one of my first RHAA contests and I had one-inch sliders on my horse. Well, it says it plain and clear in the rule book, but guess what, I didn't read it. One of the judges was nice enough to say something to me before the class. When he told me I could not show my horse in one-inch sliders, I decided to go pull out of the show. I had driven all that way and I didn't want to waste my money. After a second I asked him if I could just take the shoes off the horse. He said it would work, that I just couldn't enter the arena with those shoes on the horse. So I went and jerked off the shoes with a screwdriver and a hammer, and I had to ask the show managers to move me to the end of the class. They were nice enough to go though the trouble for me and I was able to show, but I inconvenienced everyone because I didn't take the time to read the rules. I also threw my game plan out the window because I was rushed and flustered when I went into the arena. I ended up winning the class without any shoes on my horse, but all I had to have done to have prevented the rush was read the rule book."

Don't assume that all shows have the exact same rules. Many time limits that are determined by the arena size could be different from venue to venue. Ask about time limits for each event prior to beginning the show. Then evaluate the arena to think about how much time you can spend on each element of each timed class.

"If you know that your horse is weak or that you are weak at something, you want to highlight the strong points," Lindsey says. "If he's really cowy on the end, work the cow a little bit longer. If he's good down the fence, make sure you take the time to get set up as needed to get all the points you can. Anyone can pick up some points tracking, so if you don't catch as much as you miss, at least get some points by tracking the cow."

If your horse shows well against cattle, make sure you allow yourself time to prove that ability to the judges.

THE ART OF SHOWMANSHIP— CALM, COOL, AND COLLECTED

Even though these old pros look calm, cool, and collected when they ride into the arena, that's not always an accurate portrayal of what they are going through on the inside. "I promise, the first time you show, you will ride your horse different than you ever have," Littlefield says. "You cue him faster. You pull on him more than you ever have at home. Everything gets tense. You get tight. Everything speeds up by two in the arena."

The first time Craig Haythorn competed in a Versatility Ranch Horse competition he admits he was nervous, but his anxiety was replaced by the need to do what each event asked. For him, replacing nerves with what needed to be done provided enough focus that he finished the class. The simple act of completing a class makes it easier to ride into the next one. If you have the chance to see Craig in the arena today, nerves and anxiety are not visible parts of his performance.

"I wouldn't say that I am nervous before a show, but I do get antsy," Littlefield says. "I like to compete and I get an adrenaline rush before I go into the arena. To me, the competition is exciting and I like to go up against these big names in the industry. If I didn't like it and enjoy it—if it only made me nervous—it wouldn't be fun. I wouldn't do it if it wasn't a fun way to advance our horse program."

Terry Stuart Forst adds that the only way to triumph over the anxiety is to keep trying. "You have to get out there and show your horse," she says. "Period. There is no other way to overcome it."

Once your anxiety is in check, you can focus on the ultimate goal of showing to the best of your ability. "I try to go with the attitude of not trying to beat anybody," Smith says. "I recommend that you just go do the best you can and don't be afraid to lose. Back when I was in 4-H, a man that helped haul us to shows would tell us, 'Don't go in there and beat yourself—do what you are capable of.'"

THE COLD, HARD TRUTH

Like it or not, competition means one thing—there will be winners and losers and there are always more of the latter. "When I rodeoed in high school, I was competing as a freshman against Stran Smith and Cory Koontz, who were seniors," Littlefield says. "I was about ready to quit when a man told me that I was going to have to learn to be a good loser before I could be a good winner. I choked that down. It's a simple little saying, but it's tough for people to take."

Allowing yourself to be judged is putting your pride on the line. However, the only time you aren't moving or progressing is when you aren't trying. Not winning today does not mean you will not win tomorrow.

"We have a friend from East Texas who has nice horses and wins money on them all the time," Terry Stuart Forst relates. "He came to compete in Versatility Ranch on a horse with more than two hundred performance points and expected to walk away with the top prize. He's good with cattle. The man ropes well. He's legitimate enough to do an outstanding job in the ranch classes. He got in the show situation and made some serious pilot errors in ranch cutting. He wasn't ready for crossing the bridge in ranch trail. Those little things threw him and he's of the mind-set that he'll never try it again." Forst comments that this attitude is regretful in the horse show world because some talented horses will not have the chance to show their skills. AQHA executive vice president Bill Brewer has a saying that fits this situation: winners do what losers won't.

STICKING POINTS

Every cowboy can name an element that is hardest for him. Let's eliminate the cow-related variable in cattle classes and the consensus is that the ranch trail class is the most difficult to execute. The precision and attention to detail—along with unusual obstacles— can wreak havoc on any exhibitor. "I'll tell you the hardest thing for me to get accustomed to is that trail class," Littlefield says. "Everything that you do in the trail class you do on a ranch horse at home, but you do it subconsciously. I never think about trotting over a log in the left lead when I'm in the pasture. That makes it challenging."

The "horse factor" also makes the arena challenging. Littlefield goes on to say that sometimes extensive practice doesn't always prepare your horse for the show environment. "I've seen horses that have drug everything from a baby calf to firewood to a thousand-pound cow, and you put them in that arena by themselves with cones, flags, and poles and everybody sitting around watching them and it is not the same. Then, you take the tail end of that rope and start dragging a log out behind them for no reason. You know they don't understand why they're pulling this stupid thing and I've seen them just go to blowing and snorting like they're dragging a tiger."

Depending on your point of origin, some of the trail elements may not be part of your average day. "Due to our terrain we don't cross bridges and logs or have the need to jump anything," Craig Haythorn says. "That is one reason why trail is not my favorite class. But we do drag objects—usually calves—with a rope, so it's not all out of line with our daily operation. The cattle classes are more natural for me because the cow work and roping are essential to our everyday routine on the ranch."

AFTER THE SHOW

Regardless of your horse's pedigree, age, winning record, and so forth, all horse people who have competed in a show have known on the trip home where they need to beef up their game to keep from losing points next time. Even the winners have room for improvement.

"Not every day can be perfect, but try to learn something every time you ride and you'll improve in time," Lindsey says. "All of this is simple. If you try to stay with the basics and you have the mind-set of

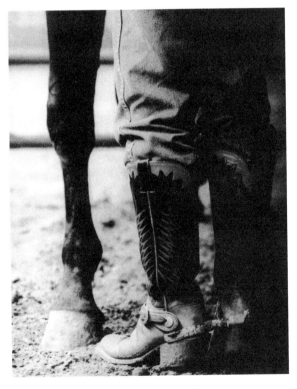

After the show, take time to reflect on your run. Going toe-to-toe with other horses is a good way to establish a standard for your performance level.

doing what is required and not getting in your horse's way, you'll do well."

If the opportunity arises, take the time to chat with the judge about how you could improve your run. Do not attempt to contest a judge's decision; simply ask about the context of your run. Following an RHAA show in Sweetwater, Texas, where Bill Smith was judging, he welcomed exhibitors to ask specific questions about their runs. He wasn't overwhelmed with questions. One young cowboy approached him to talk about his reining work. Smith told him to try to show more control of the horse without using heavy hands and to spend more time working around cattle to get a better read on them. The cowboy hadn't shown before and he asked a few more questions about his go. As the young man walked away satisfied with Smith's answers, Smith turned to me and said, "I've got somewhere I need to be, but if it only takes me giving up five minutes to answer a few questions and that person has a positive association with the ranch horse events, then my time was well spent."

Spending your time out of the arena wisely is also important to your performance. "Don't lower the bar for anything," advises Terry Stuart Forst. "If you want to be competitive, then you can go home and spend the extra time training and working on your horsemanship to become competitive. It's a never-ending process. There will always be someone out there who wants it as bad as you, has a horse as good as yours, and your drive will be what sets you apart from the other person. You can't improve by sitting in the house drinking coffee."

> Not every day can be perfect, but try to learn something
> every time you ride and you'll improve in time.
> —Kim Lindsey, Lindsey Ranch Horses

Any event that is organized, implemented, and reviewed will experience transitions, growing pains, and, ultimately, tweaking to

help it persevere through changing times and needs. In the few years since its inception, Versatility Ranch Horse events have become structured more adequately for the participants, show management, and judges. The effort to make VRH better continues.

"As with all of our classes, we are continually striving to improve the format, rules, and judging guidelines from the exhibitors' and judges' perspectives," Charlie Hemphill, AQHA senior director of shows, says. "We welcome any constructive comments that could help us make this event fit our members better. Currently, there is open discussion about incorporating an annual championship show for Versatility Ranch Horse. We're thinking about adding another division that would encompass the limited/amateur rider. At AQHA, we're always thinking ahead to provide the best experience to our members."

GET A LOOK AT THIS

AQHA offers a tutorial video called *A Return to Our Western Heritage: AQHA Versatility Ranch Horse Competition*. Hosted by *America's Horse* television front man Jeff Medders, this twenty-six-minute video gives an overview of one of AQHA's newest competitions designed for the working ranch horse. Each class is explained with tips from exhibitors who have already competed in this groundbreaking competition. Information about tack and equipment, prizes and awards, and procedures for hosting a Versatility Ranch Horse event are sections included in the video. The video concludes with a complete run from each of the five classes. The video is available through Quarter Horse Outfitters, the official distributor of AQHA educational videos, at www.quarterhorseoutfitters.com or 888-209-8322.

CHAPTER 5

HOSTING A COMPETITION

THE PROCESS

In order to receive show approval, a letter must be submitted to AQHA a minimum of ninety days prior to the event starting date, including the location of the desired event for tentative approval. The letter is reviewed within the show department at AQHA headquarters in Amarillo, Texas. The approval of a show is based on other shows already approved within a three-hundred-mile radius of the location of the desired event. If there is no known similar approved versatility ranch event on the same date within the mileage radius, the event will be approved. "We don't want to flood the market and dilute shows in the process," Charlie Hemphill, AQHA senior director of shows, says. "That's why we need to review the location. If we allowed everyone that applied to host a show, we might have four shows covering the same events and locations. That would only hurt each show because it wouldn't generate the numbers needed to make a show successfully come together."

The Versatility Ranch Horse event can be held in conjunction with other events. Show managers should budget for a $50 approval fee to be paid to AQHA.

Approved events will be listed in the Calendar of Events printed monthly in the *American Quarter Horse Journal* in the Special Events classification. Approved shows are also listed on the shows calendar found at www.aqha.com.

For those of us that make our living by working on a ranch, this competition is about us being able to go show our horses and show people what we do every day.
—*Kim Lindsey, Box P Ranch*

BEFORE THE APPLICATION

- **Discuss your goals.** Discuss what you want to accomplish with someone who has held a show in your area. Experienced show managers can help you find assistance for the day of the show. They'll also know which facilities are user friendly and provide stalls, running water, and so on.

- **Locate possible participants.** Canvass the surrounding area for interested versatility horse people. "We knew a woman who was putting on top-caliber shows in Oklahoma," Terry Stuart Forst explains. "Her first Versatility Ranch Horse show had twenty entries, including our entry. We happened to win that day and were very impressed with how well she managed all aspects of the show. Her ring help was good. Her cattle were excellent. She moved between classes in a timely manner. However, we went to several of her other shows and she was getting hard pressed to have ten entries by the summer. In fact, she had to cancel two of the shows she had on the books due to lack of interest." The time of year can cause show managers to see a dramatic swing in interest. Summer opens up a virtual catch-22 for many exhibitors. While they might have more drive to spend a day at a horse show, many have to balance that with what activities their children have scheduled.

- **Locate a cattle supplier.** Contact several cattle buyers who might be able to find the type animal you need for the date(s) of your show. Compare prices, reputation, and cattle quality to decide which supplier to use. Once a supplier is chosen, factor the necessary cattle cost estimate into your entry fee. Woodward, Oklahoma show manager Lee Ann Nickeson says in her nine months of planning, she realized that the cattle cost would be one of her greatest hurdles. After approval from AQHA, she added a safety net to her entries. "I made it clear to anyone who expressed interest that they could recoup their entry fee until a certain date," Nickeson says. "After that date, I would subtract $20 per head of cattle they would have used to cover cattle costs from their entry and send them the remainder."

AQHA requires classes that involve cattle to charge a cattle fee as part of the exhibitor's entry.

One Horse.

One Rider.

Five Events.

Now that's versatility. Discover your lifestyle.

Demonstrating versatility of a horse in five categories – ranch riding, ranch trail, ranch cutting, working ranch horse and ranch conformation. One horse and one rider must enter all five classes. Credit applied per class according to placing based on the number of horses competing in that particular class.

(806) 376-4811 www.aqha.com

AMERICAN
QUARTER
HORSE
ASSOCIATION

- **Find an announcer.** It is nice to think that you will have time to do it all the day of the show. Round up entry fees, keep scores and times, and, of course, serve as the show announcer. Don't expect this to be a reality. If you don't feel comfortable serving as the announcer for the show, designate someone to do this job. The announcer can be an integral part of keeping the show running in a timely manner. AQHA offers a sample announcer script and a VRH fact sheet to all show managers. The fact sheet is a concise way to have the announcer provide the class descriptions and other interesting facts to exhibitors and spectators.

MARKETING YOUR SHOW

The American Quarter Horse Association created the Versatility Ranch Horse competition marketing kit to assist you in promoting your event. These elements are a free service designed to help draw more exhibitors and audience members to your show.

The marketing kit includes a full-color, program-specific poster with an area to be personalized with your show information; a news release template to personalize and submit to your local newspaper and other appropriate publications; a promotion tip sheet to guide you in ways that you can garner free publicity for your show; a trophy order form to order the Lisa Perry-designed trophy, which is based on the original trophy given to the year-end, high-point award winners; and an entry list and score sheet template to be personalized and made available to spectators.

The entire kit can be downloaded from the AQHA Web site, www.aqha.com/showing/resources/vrhpromotions.html, or requested from customer service at 806-376-4811. Normal processing time is a minimum of four weeks, so AQHA recommends that you order well in advance of your event.

Appendix

Contact Information:

Details concerning organizations and associations were provided by the organizations.

Espuela Land and Cattle Company
Bill and Dana Smith
Spur, TX 79370
Phone: 806-294-5480
Bill Smith, his wife Dana, and their son Billy operate the Espuela Land and Cattle Company near Spur, Texas. The Espuela is a cow-calf operation with native grassland running around 600 English crossbred cows. The Espuela has a rich Texas ranching history as it was part of the Swenson family land holdings in West Texas. Raising solid horses is one of Smith's main goals. Toward that goal he keeps outside mares along with his own broodmare band of thirty-five mares, mostly home-raised. In 1986, Smith purchased the black stallion Black Chick Gold, of Four Sixes breeding. "Crow," as he was commonly known, helped Smith develop a widely respected breeding program. Smith has accumulated numerous titles in multiple competitions showing his Quarter Horses including the 1990 buckskin stallion Ten O Sea, 1996 dun stallion Snippys Crow and a son of Ten O Sea called "Smooth." Each July, Smith hosts a colt branding at the Espuela, offering some of the first glances at his newest foal crop.

Bill Smith brands his foal crop each July at Espuela Land and Cattle Company near Spur, Texas.

Foundation Quarter Horse Association
PO Box 1221
Mena, AZ 71953
Phone: 479-923-4768
E-mail: office@fqha.com
Web site: www.fqha.com
Office hours: 10 a.m.–2 p.m. (CST) Monday–Friday
The Foundation Quarter Horse Association is nonprofit, dedicated
to the promotion and preservation of Foundation Quarter Horses.
FQHA has the highest registration requirements of any foundation
association. Horses must be deemed eligible according to FQHA
standards before registration is approved. Only horses that have 90
percent or more Foundation Quarter Horse blood are eligible for
full FQHA registration. Horses with at least 85 percent Foundation
blood but less than 90 percent will be registered in the Appendix
section of the FQHA's registry. If your horse's foundation percent-
age meets FQHA standards, it will qualify for registration in all other
foundation groups.

Haythorn Land and Cattle Company
193 Haythorn Dr.
Arthur, NE 69121
Phone: 308-355-4000
Fax: 308-355-4444
E-mail: Haythorn@lakemac.net
Web site: www.haythorn.com
The Haythorn Land and Cattle Company is known as the largest
breeder of Quarter Horses in the United States, and the second largest
in the world. Winner of the coveted Inaugural AQHA Best Remuda
Award, Haythorn Land and Cattle Company is a working ranch
breeding Black Angus, Hereford, and longhorn cattle as well as
foundation-bred Quarter Horses. On average, the ranch keeps five

Craig Haythorn's boots.

hundred horses on hand as a result of its breeding program. Day-to-day ranching activities incorporate the horses ridden by working cowboys. Haythorn Land and Cattle Company is made up of more than ninety thousand acres of leased and deeded land spanning three counties. The ranch is located seventeen miles north of Ogallala, Nebraska.

Iowa Ranch Horse Association

Susie Spry, secretary
2717 Witmer St.
Des Moines, IA 50310
Phone: 515-279-1036
E-mail: susies@iowaranchhorse.com
Web site: www.iowaranchhorse.com
The Iowa Ranch Horse Association is a group of more than three hundred horse enthusiasts who want to enjoy their horses in an entirely different type of competitive atmosphere. Designed with the beginner in mind, IRHA frequently holds clinics in conjunction with shows. IRHA is about more than just competing. IRHA members take pride in their association. You don't have to compete in the shows to be considered a "real" member. The organization is dedicated to promoting well-broke, reliable working horses and the members share a love for that true equine athlete, but owning a horse is not required for active participation in this group. The IRHA is led by a board of directors, consisting of officers and eight district representatives.

Lindsey Ranch Horses/Box P Ranch

Kim Lindsey
3250 CR 350
Jayton, TX 79528
Phone: 806-254-2050
Fax: 806-254-2008
E-mail: klindsey@caprock-spur.com
As an employee of the Box P Ranch, Kim Lindsey has the opportunity to expose her horses to daily ranch work, which prepares horses and rider for the ranch-based horse events. Lindsey takes an active role in AQHA, SHOT, and RHAA events. In 2003, she rode the top cowboy class horse, Dozen Plus Freckles, in the Best of America's

Horse honor. This acknowledges the American Quarter Horse and its ability to compete in versatile events.

While Lindsey spends most of her time on the ranch working and checking cattle, she also finds time to give riding lessons and help pass on her horse knowledge to others. She and her husband have a registered Angus herd they run on the ranch.

Kim Lindsey adjusts the brow band of Sunnys First Pauli after a full practice session on the Box P Ranch near Jayton, Texas. The 1999 bay gelding is by Pauli O Lena and out of Taris Sunny Miss. Lindsey competes on the gelding in AQHA, RHAA, RCHA, and SHOT, and uses him for everyday ranch work.

Butch's saddle

Nevada All-Around Working Cow Horse

Liz Younger, president/owner

223 Marsh Ave.

Reno, NV 89509

Phone: 775-329-4200

Fax: 775-329-4283

E-mail: liz@youngeragency.com

Web site: www.youngeragency.com

The Nevada All-Around Working Cow Horse contests are designed to demonstrate and perpetuate the traditional working cow horse. This contest has been in place for more than a decade. The all-around is for bridle horses only. The open divisions are for bridle-, hackamore-, and snaffle-bit horses. The Nevada All-Around Working Cow Horse Championship is open to any rider with no geographic limitations. Awards are given to the top working cow horse, top rancher (must have a registered brand), working cowboy/cowgirl, high-point family, and high-point ranch.

The Pitchfork Land and Cattle Company
PO Box 120
Guthrie, TX 79236
Phone: 806-284-2223
Fax: 806-284-2675
Contact: Bob Moorhouse, manager
E-mail: Bob@ThePitchforkRanch.com
Web site: www.ThePitchforkRanch.com

Pitchfork Ranch manager Bob Moorhouse, shows 1999 sorrel gelding Sancies Dynamite (Dynamite Badger X Sancie Leo Freckles) in the Ranch Horse Association of America Junior Class in May 2004. This performance earned the pair from Guthrie, Texas, second place in the RHAA finals.

Established in 1883, the Pitchfork's operations span around 180,000 acres in two states and more than a century of continuous operation primarily under one family. The home ranch includes 165,000 acres in Dickens and King Counties near the town of Guthrie. The ranch also has a satellite operation in Kansas. With around five thousand mother cows grazing the home ranch, the cowboys have the opportunity to work the range horseback in a manner very similar to the first Pitchfork cowboys. The Pitchfork crew can often be found riding horses that are a symbol of the ranch—the signature "Pitchfork Gray." The gray horse with a black mane and tail is a color combo often found in the Pitchfork remuda. The ranch's remuda consists of approximately fifty broodmares, 150 saddle horses, and five stallions.

Ranch Cutting Horse Association
560 Wilson Ranch Road
Holliday, TX 76366
Phone: 940-525-4270 or 940-631-4490
Web site: www.ranchcutters.com
The Ranch Cutting Horse Association (RCHA) was formed in 1998 to fill a void left by the overspecialization in the horse industry. For years the ranches used cutting events as a showcase and marketing tool for the ranch and their trained horses. The RCHA-sanctioned events are open to any working ranch's family or an employee of the ranch riding true ranch horses that are used for day-to-day activities on the ranch. The goal of the RCHA is to promote an enjoyable experience for all involved and to help the ranches showcase their ranch horses. Members of the RCHA hail from more than sixty different ranches and represent almost 2.5 million acres of land, more than fifty thousand head of mother cows, and nearly 150,000 yearlings.

George Beggs IV of Post, Texas, examines the herd during a Ranch Cutting Horse Association class. Beggs is riding Becaco Echo, a 1990 brown gelding, by Doctor Echo and out of Becaco Twoonese Last. Becaco stands for Beggs Cattle Company and has been part of the registered name of all Beggs ranch horses for the past twenty years or more.

Ranch Horse Association of America
PO Box 7723
Abilene, TX 79608
Phone: 325-529-5637
E-mail: raylene@rhaa.org
Web site: www.rhaa.org

The RHAA was formed in 1998 to promote the qualities and characteristics of the ultimate working ranch horse, while providing a means of competition to show these ranch horses. The RHAA sanctions local working ranch horse competitions, provides a uniform set of rules, qualifies working ranch horse competition judges, and promotes uniformity and consistency in judging. The RHAA seeks to accomplish these goals while maintaining traditional Western influence with historic Western sportsmanship and a cowboy ethic. A membership application can be downloaded from the RHAA Web site. RHAA National Finals occur each May in Abilene during the Western Heritage Classic Ranch Rodeo.

Rocky Mountain Quarter Horse Association
Ranch Horse Program
4701 Marion St., Ste. 318
Denver, CO 80216
Phone: 303-296-1143
Contact: Dave Currin 719-481-9311
Web site: www.rmqha.com/versatility_ranch_horse.htm
The Rocky Mountain Quarter Horse Association has developed a program for riders interested in participating in the Versatility Ranch Horse competition at a level other than that of AQHA pointed shows. This program has as its primary purpose the enjoyment of education and competition without the pressures of "big time" showing. Realizing that many of the folks who have an interest in the VRH have never even acquired the various skills of the five different classes that make up the VRH event, RMQHA features several skill levels for beginners to start with until they feel confident with their overall progress to advance to the next level. With two levels for the beginner or novice, two levels for the amateur, and one for the open rider, RMQHA feels it truly has a program that riders can enjoy while developing their skills in the VRH discipline. The plan further allows participants to earn year-end recognition for their efforts throughout the year. With a series of clinics designed to improve one's skills and friendly competitions in which to test those skills, RMQHA has developed an awards program that recognizes the achievements of all levels of riders who participate.

Stock Horse of Texas
B. F. Yeates
Stock Horse of Texas Association
3708 E. 29th St., PMB #101
Bryan, TX 77802
Phone: 979-846-4538
E-mail: info@stockhorse.org
Web site: www.stockhorse.org
The Stock Horse of Texas (SHOT) program is a partnership between Texas horse users, breeders, ranchers, associations, organizations, stock shows, sales companies, and colleges, which is facilitated through the Texas Cooperative Extension Service and Texas A&M University System. SHOT was created in 1998 by an industry task force of breeders, ranchers, organization representatives, and educators. Membership is open to all stock horse breeds and Western stock horse enthusiasts, regardless of age, sex, location, or economic circumstances.

SHOT strives to meet the present and emerging needs of the Texas Western stock horse industry by continuously strengthening the knowledge of interested members. SHOT offers educational clinics for horses and riders, hosts competition to display stock horse skills, provides private treaty and public auction opportunities, and coordinates objectives with collegiate horse programs.

7S Stuart Ranch
Terry Stuart Forst, general manager
Chris Littlefield, horse division manager and trainer
PO Box 247
Waurika, OK 73573
Phone: 580-228-3272
Fax: 580-228-3273
E-mail: stuartrn@texhoma.net
Web site: www.stuartranch.com

Riding for Stuart Ranch, Chris Littlefield and stallion Real Gun circle a calf during a 2003 working cow horse competition in Oklahoma City. Real Gun is by Playgun and out of Miss War Chips. In 2004, Real Gun was named AQHA's World Show Superhorse after taking second in senior working cow horse, third in senior heeling, and fifth in senior calf roping under the hand of Littlefield.

The R T Stuart Ranch LLC is the oldest family-owned ranch in Oklahoma. The Stuart Ranch consists of more than forty thousand acres of native grass and runs an average of twenty broodmares. It was designated as an Oklahoma Centennial Ranch and was awarded the AQHA/Bayer Best Remuda Award in 1995. The ranch has produced numerous world champions, including the 1995 Superhorse, Genuine Redbud. Real Gun, a 1999 gray stallion, took home top honors at the 2004 AQHA World Championship Show, winning the Superhorse award. Every foal raised on Stuart Ranch spends its first two years in the pasture, then goes on to work on the ranch, gathering, sorting, and branding cattle. Only then will a horse have the opportunity to prove it can compete in the show ring. Stuart-raised horses have earned points in numerous AQHA events including Versatility Ranch Horse, Western pleasure, calf roping, heading, heeling, working cow horse, cutting, reining, halter, hunter under saddle, equitation, barrel racing, pole bending, and trail. Currently, the ranch is standing stallions Real Gun (Playgun X Miss War Chips) and Seven S Zanaday who is by Zan Parr Bar and out of Stuart-raised mare May Day Hobby. Daily work on the Stuart Ranch requires horses with athleticism, cow sense, and stamina.

Tongue River Ranch
HC 2 Box 20
Paducah, TX 79248
Phone: 806-596-4641
Fax: 806-596-4791
E-mail: patti@tongueriverranch.com
Web site: www.TongueRiverRanch.com
Tongue River Ranch, owned by Millard Morris of DeRidder, Louisiana, is located in King, Cottle, Dickens, and Motley Counties in West Texas. It covers ninety thousand acres surrounding Dumont, Texas. The ranch gets its name from its location on the South Pease

Donald Rutledge and Stepped In Sonny take part in a ranch horse cutting event as part of the ranch-based competitions during the Western Heritage Classic in Abilene, Texas, each May.

River (River of Many Tongues) in northwestern Texas. S. M. Swenson bought the ranch in the late 1800s from the railroads and operated it as the Tongue River division of the famous Swenson Ranch. The Tongue River is part of the South Pease River, but according to legend, because of the many languages spoken among the settlers and traders, the Indians named the area "The River Of Many Tongues," which was later shortened to Tongue River. The Tongue

River cowboys stay horseback for most of their day-to-day work, which involves managing the care for fourteen hundred mother cows and twelve hundred yearlings pastured at the ranch. TRR keeps approximately seventy broodmares in its remuda and offer breedings to four of the ranch's studs.

Western Heritage Classic Ranch Rodeo
Expo Center of Taylor County
1700 Hwy. 36
Abilene, TX 79602
Phone: 325-677-4376
Web site: www.WesternHeritageClassic.com
It began in 1985 when a few local cowboys formed teams to compete in authentic ranch activities that involved a scoring system used to determine which was the best working ranch. Today, it is an organized event called the Western Heritage Classic, which allows working ranches to show their stuff in a two-day competition that includes bronc riding, wild cow milking, team penning, team roping, and calf branding.

The Western Heritage Classic is now recognized internationally. Held on the grounds of the Taylor County Expo Center in Abilene, Texas, the three-day event's showcase is the ranch rodeo. Visitors can also tour the World's Largest Bit and Spur Show, dine from the offerings of the Chuckwagon Cookoff, take part in the Matched Horse Races, enter their children in the children's stick horse rodeo, delight the senses with cowboy poets and Western artisans, and witness ranch horse clinics and a giant Western parade. All of these events add to the wide range that the Western Heritage Classic offers spectators each year.

In 1998 the Ranch Horse Association of America added its national finals for the Working Ranch Horse competition to the

Western Heritage Classic schedule. During the Saturday night performance of the WHC Ranch Rodeo, the top two finalists compete for the national title. Historic ranches are able to offer their ranch horses in Saturday's WHC Invitational Ranch Horse Sale.

Working Ranch Cowboy Association
PO Box 7765
Amarillo, TX 79114
Phone: 806-374-9722
Fax: 806-374-9724
E-mail: wrca@arn.net
Web site: www.wrca.org
WRCA was organized in 1995 by men and women across the United States who were either active in ranching or had a ranching background. Their goal was to create a type of support group for the ranching cowboy, similar to support groups offered by other professions. The WRCA considers itself to be a representative and defender of cowboys and cowgirls.

The WRCA was created in Amarillo with two hundred founding members. Many members were ranch owners, managers, and cowboys, but some were people who believed in the WRCA ideals. The WRCA Web site explains that all of its members believe in the ideals and work ethic of the working ranch cowboy and the desire to keep the Western heritage alive in this ever-changing world. It is the desire of the WRCA to see the organization grow throughout the world, supporting the ranch cowboy in every country. It believes that all people share the same needs, ideals, and work ethics, regardless of nationality.

Index

divisions, 8–9
double judged/double point
status, 34

E
Espuela Example, 49–50
Espuela Land and Cattle
Company, 49–50, 105
establishment of, 3–7
experience, 32–33

F
foot examination, 55–56
Foundation Quarter Horse
Association, 107
Four Sixes Ranch, 4

G
gaits, 50–52
gate work, 53–54
geldings, 30, 32
general rules, 23–24
ground tying, 57–59
Gunnin To Play, 36

H
hackamores, 81
halters, 21
Haythorn Land and Cattle
Company, 36, 107–8
head set, 52
headstalls, 21
hobbling, 57–59
horse factor, 94

horse sales, 38–39, 41–42
horsemanship, 44–45
horses
desired characteristics, 32–36
purchasing, 30, 32, 38–39,
41–42, 45
selection of, 25–28
selling, 42, 44–45
hosting competitions
details of, 99–101, 103
marketing and, 103
process of, 99–100

I
Ima Eddie Hancock, 5
Incentive Fund, 8
industrialization, 3
Invitational Ranch Horse Show
and Sale, 41
Iowa Ranch Horse Association,
109–10

J
Joe Don Hancock, 5

L
land development, 3
lead changes, 67–68
leather, 21
left lead, 67
leg protection, 21, 23
Lindsey Ranch Horses, 110
Little Playgun, 4
log pulling, 54–55